The
PERFECT
MEMO

JOAN MINNINGER, Ph.D.

THE PERFECT MEMO

DOUBLEDAY

NEW YORK LONDON TORONTO SYDNEY AUCKLAND

PUBLISHED BY DOUBLEDAY
a division of Bantam Doubleday Dell Publishing Group, Inc.
666 Fifth Avenue, New York, New York 10103

DOUBLEDAY and the portrayal of an anchor
with a dolphin are trademarks of Doubleday,
a division of Bantam Doubleday Dell
Publishing Group, Inc.

DEDICATION

To my son Christopher,
a premier strategist.

ACKNOWLEDGMENTS

Special heartfelt appreciation to Eleanor Knowles Dugan, C. Delos Putz,
and Leigh Dickerson Davidson for their extraordinary crafting expertise
which added so much to this book; to Becky Gordon for her amazing
editorial skill; to Michael Larsen, who saw its possibilities and made
the perfect match; and to John Duff, always a pleasure to work with,
who said "Yes!"

Library of Congress Cataloging-in-Publication Data
Minninger, Joan.
The perfect memo / Joan Minninger. — 1st ed.
      p.   cm.
1. Business writing.   2. Memorandums.   I. Title.
      HF5718.3.M56   1990
651.7'55—dc20   89–28154
                                                          CIP
ISBN 0-385-26773-8
Copyright © 1990 by Joan Minninger, Ph.D.

Book Design by Donna Sinisgalli

Contents

The
PERFECT
MEMO

What You Need to Start Writing

You are about to commit an unnatural act. It is called memo writing, and it defies all the ancient traditions and inborn instincts of human communication.

From the *Aeneid* to "Goldilocks," the natural exchange of information has been based on presenting events in a progression through time. Start at the beginning. Stop at the end. Nothing could be simpler or more logical.

This "once upon a time" approach positions us comfortably for the drama ahead. It's soothing and traditional . . . and absolutely wrong for memos. Once-upon-a-time may be great for storytelling and a valuable way to collect your thoughts and opinions on a subject, but it turns in-boxes into nightmares and sabotages your ideas and directives.

In 1978, the executive vice president of a large manufacturing firm called me for help with the company's in-house writing. "I used to read through the contents of my in-box on the train commuting between New York City and Tarrytown," he said, "but every day it's getting worse. The memos are getting longer and more confusing. You've got to help. I don't want to have to move to Schenectady!"

The first thing I did for his company took less than a minute and subtracted hundreds of hours from his yearly reading time: I suggested a small change in the company memo form. A single line was added where the writers checked off *why* they were writing. This helped the readers enormously, preparing them for what was ahead. Not surprisingly, it also helped the writers clarify their own thinking and kept them on track. I've done regular writing seminars for their management-level personnel ever since, demonstrating how Perfect Memos benefit both the reader and the writer.

Why should a busy executive take the time and energy to learn to write well? Because *writing is behavior!* Your writing represents you and how you feel about others just as much as your appearance, manners, and business skills do. Weak, flabby, confused writing is boring, ineffective, and costly. It can even be dangerous.

Fortunately you don't have to be a CEO to write like one, to present complex ideas, issues, or instructions simply, forcefully, and persuasively. Yes, there *are* effective business people who have others do all their writing. There are also pop stars who have others sing, dance, or play musical instruments for them on the screen. But genuine stardom comes from genuine performances and communicating is usually part of doing business.

Fortunately, clear, powerful writing is not difficult when you know a few simple rules . . . and it's a lot easier than doing a backflip while playing a saxophone.

HOW TO USE THIS BOOK

This book contains disguised versions of *real* in-house documents—memos, reports, proposals, minutes, and instructions—in a before-and-after format. These misguided gems have been collected during my eighteen years of Executive Writing seminars for Fortune 500 companies. I am grateful to their authors and to the seminar participants who have helped to hone them to their present sleekness.

The material in this book is arranged in three sections:

    I.   What You Need to Start Writing

    II. Perfect Memos: The Seven Keys to Clear Writing

    III. Other In-House Communications

You can use this material in two different ways. You can take full advantage of this book, doing all the assignments. You can also use it as a quick overview and reference guide.

The Two-Hour Speed Sprint
Read the book straight through, stopping only to do the four assignments labeled "Speed-Sprint Compulsory."

The Twenty-Four-Hour Intensive
Read the book, answering all the questions and doing all the assignments.

ABOUT MEMOS

Even if you put this book down forever afterward, if you read this section you will learn two things that will double the impact of your business writing and more than repay the cost of this book. They are incredibly simple. They are:

Rule 1. *Good structure promotes good substance.*

When you use an organized structure it is hard(er) to fill it with muddled, muddy thinking. As a starter, many of my corporate clients have found that the clarity of their in-house communications was vastly improved when they instituted a preprinted memo form that asked the writers to identify *why* they were writing:

```
This memo is for:
[ ] action    [ ] decision    [ ] information
```

This incredibly simple device positions both the writers and the readers, and saves their companies hundreds of hours and thousands of dollars a year.

Rule 2. *Write for the convenience of the reader.*

What does the reader want to know? What does the reader *need* to know? Delete everything else and you have made a tremendous advance in engaging the heart, mind, and eyeballs of your reader.

Why do we resist reading most of the things that cross our desks every day? Because they are boring time-wasters! Imagine a typical once-upon-a-time piece of business writing. First the writer describes how he noticed the problem, then how he discussed it with Joe who suggested he call Jane who said he should write to you, then how the problem started, what has been happening, what may happen in the future, and, way down at the bottom of the last page, what he thinks ought to be done about it.

Meanwhile the readers, if they are still reading, are frantically asking, "Why are you telling me all this?" The writer didn't write for the convenience of the reader. He started at the beginning and went step-by-step to the end.

"But that's how I think!"

Of course, it is. You wouldn't be an intelligent, reasoning human being if you didn't. And it's okay to write like that . . . just don't send it. You'll learn how to craft this exploratory writing into Perfect Memos with the Two-Phase Technique in the next part of this section, "How to Write the Perfect Memo."

All in the Family

It has been estimated that 70 percent of business writing never leaves the office. It simply relays requests and information between people and departments within the company. This form of business writing is usually called a memo—it can also go by other names like:

report	bulletin
proposal	directive
minutes	information sheet
instruction	brief
study	guideline
summary	job description
abstract	performance evaluation
prospectus	position statement
digest	feasibility study
analysis	progress report
profile	audit report
manual	fiscal report

There are special sections in this book about writing minutes, reports, proposals, and instructions.

Writing the Company Language

Many companies are miniature cultures with their own customs and taboos. Some of these customs and taboos have been formalized into a *Manual of Procedures* and some are individual idiosyncrasies like "Mr. Blat hates men who wear striped ties." If Mr. Blat is a valuable employee, his personal bias may be tolerated. If he's the boss, it may eventually become the company dress code.

A company's style of writing takes on the same cultural sanctity. Nothing pleases CEOs more than to see their own words and style coming back at them, no matter how byzantine. It demonstrates loyalty and a common identity. People naturally try to identify themselves with a group by adopting its customs of speech, dress, mannerisms—and writing style. Therefore, changes in company writing style usually need to come down from the top.

But even if you're not a CEO, don't despair. You can still gain major personal benefits by mastering the principles of the Perfect Memo:

You will be more easily understood and therefore have more chance of gaining cooperation.

You will hone your organizing ability by learning about how to organize your writing.

You will be better able to decode the confusing, obscure communications that cross your desk.

In some large companies, the style has been set by tradition ("We've always done it that way") or by decree (*Manual of Procedures*) or it may have just "grow'd" like Topsy. How the style evolved is less important than how effective it is. A brisk, casual style may be perfect for one organization while a formal, impersonal, detached style may work superbly for another. Just remember:

Style shouldn't affect content.

You can be warm or distant, conciliatory or disapproving, eager or unimpressed, and still not sacrifice clarity.

Surviving the Memo Jungle

A company's writing style shows more about how it works than all its advertising and public relations. In an organization where people are extraordinarily clear about their goals, their roles, and their procedures, the focus is on "what do you want done?" People are action-oriented and their memos reflect this.

At the other extreme are companies where every action is a "favor," asked for with great ceremony. These are frequently companies that started as small, friendly organizations and expanded quickly. Many people still aren't clear about who is supposed to do what and so requests are couched in pleasant and tentative language:

> I hesitate to ask you, but if you could and would and did, I'd be so grateful.

Or worse:

> There may just be a problem and if some unspecified person decides that there is, then another unspecified person might try to do something about it . . . maybe.

These companies are usually people-oriented and want to treat everyone with great sensitivity, an admirable objective, but this kind of writing will eventually erode morale and waste a lot of time and money. They don't realize that vagueness can be offensive too.

The Emotional Aspects of Memos

When you write a memo, you probably are doing one of the following:

- asking for something
- confirming a verbal request
- responding to a request (positively or negatively)
- offering information (which may be criticized or rejected)

Ironically, memos can require even more diplomacy than press releases or letters that project the company image to the outside world. Memos are domestic in nature, dealing with the home front. We can bring a lot of emotional debris to our requests of coworkers, along with our fear of refusal, of losing prestige, or of being exposed to criticism. Yet few people in business can afford *never* to communicate what they are doing or thinking, what they need and expect and oppose.

The subtle but crucial relationships among employees can make or break a company, and office politics sometimes rival those of a banana republic. Memos represent social as well as business "glue" for those relationships.

Each culture has evolved a code of conduct for communication between its members. The most elaborate and variable codes usually involve business relationships. In some societies, a lengthy social exchange of hours or even days is necessary before business can be discussed. Anything less would be unspeakably crude.

In this country we've speeded up the social preliminaries, but they're still there. When we approach business associates, we usually greet them, ask how they are doing, how their family is doing, or what they've been up to. We use these preliminaries to establish rapport before going on to business.

Many of us carry these conversational traditions over into our business writing. We try to enhance our requests and soften our refusals with elaborate expositions and lengthy explanations. We think we are being polite, but frequently we are just being obscure.

We're going to show you how to abandon the baggage of conversational traditions when you sit down to write. Business memos can be clear *and* kind, direct *and* friendly, short *and* persuasive.

Technical Writing

Experts disagree about whether there is such a thing as "technical writing," but most people agree that there are definite characteristics that divide "scientific" and "imaginative" writing:

SCIENTIFIC WRITING
- can only be interpreted one way
- is logical
- deals with facts
- connects causes and effects

IMAGINATIVE WRITING
- can (and even should) be interpreted in more than one way
- is stimulating
- deals with ideas
- points out relationships

Technology requires both imagination and logic. Therefore, good "technical writing" has the same characteristics as good business writing. It should have only one meaning (unless you want or need to be imprecise). It should also favorably stimulate the person receiving it (unless you deliberately want a negative response).

What About "Memo English"?

The "enclosed please find" school of business writing is fortunately fading, but a new style of jargon is springing up in its place. We call it "Memo English." One executive got the following:

> Reference mine of 3/10 and action. Copy me.

The writer wanted to receive a photocopy of correspondence or work orders to confirm that his previous instructions, sent on March 10, had been carried out. Whether you choose to write like this or not, you'll probably be seeing a lot of it in the next few years.

This might be called the "Verbing of America." Nouns are being turned into verbs and adjectives into nouns at an incredible rate. Public officials now conjugate the verbs "to impact," "to context," "to potential," and "to decision." The writer usually sees Memo English as more succinct and dynamic, but it can also be longer and less clear.

English is a magnificent language, capable of infinite poetry, brevity, versatility, and adaptability. If we treat it with love and a modicum of respect, it will do the same for us.

HOW TO WRITE THE PERFECT MEMO

Your preliminary once-upon-a-time writing is invaluable for the insights it gives you. Whatever you do, don't stop doing it. But whatever you do, don't send it.

Instead, use the Two-Phase Technique to divide your business writing into two parts:

- the Exploratory Phase
- the Crafting Phase

This is the way to conquer and organize difficult, complex, or confusing material.

Where to Start—The Exploratory Phase

Sit down and write the most elaborate once-upon-a-time story you can. Explore every facet. Digress. Develop. Dazzle. Say everything you ever wanted to say on the subject.

Jot down what you need to write about. Allow yourself to write whatever comes into your head with no attempt to organize it. Gather all you know that is relevant. Don't let anyone criticize it at this point, not even yourself. Don't let yourself imagine an audience for what you are saying. Forget what you think someone else may want to hear. This writing belongs to you. If you get stuck, start with one of these phrases:

I know . . .	I will . . .
I think . . .	I won't . . .
I feel . . .	I can . . .
I want . . .	I can't . . .

Use whatever pronoun you need: I-you-he-she-we-they. Just keep writing. Don't stop to judge. If a voice inside you starts nagging with "that's not good enough," reply like the skillful administrator you are, "Of course it's not and I'm glad you're perceptive enough to recognize that. I'll need your talents later. Have my secretary pencil you in for Tuesday on your way out." Right now you are creating the raw materials from which you will structure the final "Reader Edition."

Writer's Block? If you find yourself freezing up when you start to write, here's a foolproof trick for you. Set a timer for ten minutes and try Continuous Writing. Put your pen on the paper and draw continuous loops over and over until words come to you. Don't evaluate what you're writing. If you prefer typing, get a roll of shelf paper or a folded pack of computer paper and position it behind your typewriter so it will feed through continuously. Then type "fjfjfj" over and over until words come. Having a ten-minute limit makes it easier to start, and almost no one can stop when the timer goes off.

How to Finish—The Crafting Phase

Now that you have let yourself know what you are thinking in the Exploratory Phase, you are ready to pick out what you want to tell your reader. This is your Crafting Phase.

Step 1. *Underline what your reader needs to know.*

Go back over what you have written and put a line under everything your reader needs to know.

Step 2. *Decide why you are writing.*

What is the purpose of your communication? Write this down at the top of a sheet of paper:
　　The purpose of this memo is to _____.
Tell your readers in the first sentence why you are writing. Define their position for them so they know if you want them to act, decide, recommend, or simply to be aware of the information you are sending. Don't make them read on and on, muttering "Why are you telling me all this?"
　　For example:

> *The purpose of this memo is to* explain why we have three more employees on the Focus Project than are provided for in the budget— 20 actual versus 17 budgeted.

Or:

> *The purpose of this memo is to* tell you how to use the new shipping procedures.

(Once you are used to making a frame of reference for yourself as well as for the reader, you can drop the opening part of the sentence and revert to more direct English.)

Step 3. *Take what you have underlined and divide it into separate topics and issues.*

If your raw material covers more than one point, pull out all the underlined information from your exploratory work and organize it into categories. If the material is lengthy, you may want to sort it into separate file folders or word processor files with topic labels.

Step 4. *Write a heading for each action, issue, or topic.*

Let the reader know immediately what you are talking about with an accurate and informative heading: "Your

New Medical Benefits" (not "Benefits"); "When to Deliver Parts" (not "Timetable"). Writing good headings is covered in the next section.

Step 5. *Number each issue in order of importance to the reader.*

What does your reader need to know first? Then what? For instance, the most important issue for the organization may be how much money will be saved by a new procedure, but the most important issue for the Receiving Department clerk is what he has to do, when, and how.

Step 6. *Put the most important thing first, then number two, number three, etc.*

Take that sheet of paper with the purpose of your communication at the top. That is probably the title of your memo or report. Start with the most important thing you have to say. Then go on down your list—you have already numbered them.

Information that is strictly background or support goes at the end so that your audience can read it if they are interested. Use attachments if necessary. Don't dilute the purpose of your writing. Keep the first page crisp. If your memo runs more than one page, you may want to state the purpose on the first page and attach clearly labeled schedules, charts, and lists.

For example:

Summer vacations may be taken between May 30 and August 29. Schedules and pay charts are attached.

However, don't try to make simple communications look more important by attaching unnecessary pages. They are a waste of paper and probably won't be read. (If the whole package looks too intimidating, your first page may not be read either.)

In the next section, "Perfect Memos: The Seven Keys to Clear Writing," you will learn the simple characteristics of the Perfect Memo.

Perfect Memos: The Seven Keys to Clear Writing

A popular symbol of business prestige is the key to the executive washroom, but these seven keys to the Perfect Memo can take you into the *board*room. They are the keys for transforming diffused, confused, unwieldy prose into crisp, clear communications.

Don't be put off by the number seven. You won't have to go over everything you write seven times to make it work. These seven techniques overlap and run together so logically that once you're aware of them, you'll think of them as one mighty tool.

1. **Clear Subject**
   What are you writing about? Is that clear from your heading or first sentence? Are you writing about more than one thing?

2. **Purpose Up Front**
   Why are you writing? Do you need action? A decision? Are you giving information? What is the most important thing you are saying?

3. **Conclusion Up Front**
   What have you decided or recommended?

4. **Headings**
Can you bunch similar issues or tasks together and then cook up useful labels to announce them?

5. **Verbs**
What do you want done? Use active, transitive verbs.

6. **Short Paragraphs and Sentences**
Avoid choking chunks of type. Is your writing easy to read?

7. **Attachments**
Will your writing be easier to understand if you put background information, schedules, instructions, charts, etc. in attachments?

Section II of this book consists of original memos illustrating each of the seven keys above. The original memo appears on the left-hand page. Follow the instructions on the *What to Do* page opposite it. Then turn to the next page to see what we did to improve the original and to see the rewrite.

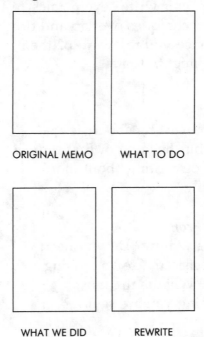

ORIGINAL MEMO   WHAT TO DO

WHAT WE DID   REWRITE

CHAPTER 1

Clear Subject

 What are you writing about? Is that clear from your subject heading? Does the content of your memo match the subject heading?

Create a Clear Subject Heading

What is the news? Write a clear, accurate heading, alerting your reader to what is coming.

Avoid generic headings like "Shipping Department" or "Barton Contract." What *about* the shipping department? Your subject heading should be specific:

NOT: Shipping Department

BUT: Effect of Shipping Dept. Move on Your
      February Deliveries

OR   New Shipping Procedures Start Friday,
      May 1

NOT: Inventory Schedule

BUT: Return Your Inventory Forms by May 1

Be sure to frame and emphasize the information from the reader's point of view. We all pay more attention to what affects us personally.

The subject heading of your memo is like a newspaper headline. It is the first clue your readers have to why you are writing and why they are reading.

Don't Mix Your Messages

- Does your subject heading describe one thing, when the memo is actually about something else?
- Are you trying to discuss several unrelated things under an umbrella heading? (Sometimes separate memos are more efficient.)
- Are you trying to sneak in a recommendation or complaint disguised as a report? (You may consider this "diplomacy," but often it is either annoying or confusing to the reader.)
- Are you 100 percent clear in your own mind why you are writing? (If you're not, your reader may not be either.)

Avoid Surprises

Lyndon Johnson made quite a stir when he mentioned casually at the end of a routine speech that he would not run for reelection. Burying the real news can be great for dramatic effect, as it was in this case, but it can just as easily backfire in a memo or report. The hurried reader, given an incorrect frame of reference by the subject heading and preceding material, may misinterpret your main point or overlook it altogether.

Simple, clear communication will:

save errors

save energy

save time

save money

TO: All Concerned   DATE: June 19, 1998

FROM: Josephine Baker, Book Division

SUBJECT: August '98 Sales Conference

According to the schedule attached, all materials for sales conference presentations are due July 12th—not too far off. Will you please begin to think about and gather the materials we will need to shoot for the slide show?

It is my understanding that we will continue using the style we did last conference: one slide with jacket and author photo, so for all titles we will need an author photo. Exceptions would be if the photo the author sent in is unusable, or if it doesn't make any sense to show the author's face, or if there are more than one author and they're not all in the same photo.

Additional slides are done only if they will truly help support the presentation: anything that needs to be read thoroughly should instead be included in the accompanying brochure. Exceptions to this rule are slides of competing titles, previous successful books (with sales figures!), press clippings of note, quotes, etc. Remember that we need to try to keep it all at a minimum to keep a good flow.

You can begin sending things to me at any time—I will begin putting them in order for the show—but everything will need to be in my office by the morning of July 12th, unless we've agreed otherwise.

If you have any questions, please call me. Hope this memo reads!

Thanks.

CC: JD, JB, PK, TMD, JEF, KL, BP, JK, JC, MF, JL

WHAT TO DO

This is a charming and chatty talking-to-myself memo. Since it is going out to eleven people, it would be a lot easier for them to grasp if the subject were clearer and the requested items were broken out.

1. Suggest a new subject for this memo.

2. Put a check next to each thing the reader is being asked to send to the writer.

3. Put an "X" next to each thing that represents an exception to the writer's requirements.

TO: All Concerned   DATE: June 19, 1998

FROM: Josephine Baker, Book Division

SUBJECT: August '98 Sales Conference

According to the schedule attached, all materials for sales conference presentations are due July 12th—not too far off. Will you please begin to think about and gather the materials we will need to shoot for the slide show?

It is my understanding that we will continue using the style we did last conference: one slide with jacket and author photo, so for all titles we will need an author photo. Exceptions would be if the photo the author sent in is unusable, or if it doesn't make any sense to show the author's face, or if there are more than one author and they're not all in the same photo.

Additional slides are done only if they will truly help support the presentation: anything that needs to be read thoroughly should instead be included in the accompanying brochure. Exceptions to this rule are slides of competing titles, previous successful books (with sales figures!), press clippings of note, quotes, etc. Remember that we need to try to keep it all at a minimum to keep a good flow.

You can begin sending things to me at any time—I will begin putting them in order for the show—but everything will need to be in my office by the morning of July 12th, unless we've agreed otherwise.

If you have any questions, please call me. Hope this memo reads!

Thanks.

CC: JD, JB, PK, TWD, JEF, KL, BP, JK, JC, MF, JL

ANSWERS

1. The subject is the July 12 deadline for sales conference slides.

2. Items one through five in the rewrite represent the things the reader is being asked to send the writer.

3. The exceptions are highlighted in the rewrite under item two and under the heading "Other Information."

•   •   •   •

OUR REWRITE

SUBJECT CHANGED FROM   August '98 Sales Conference

TO   July 12 Deadline— Sales Conference Slides

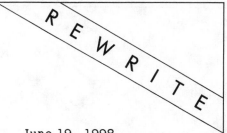

```
      TO:     All Concerned        DATE:    June 19, 1998

    FROM:     Josephine Baker,      CC:    JD   JB   PK   MF
              Book Division                TMD  JEF  KL   JL
                                           BP   JK   JC

 SUBJECT:     July 12 Deadline—Sales Conference Slides

    FOR:      [X] action    [ ] decision    [ ] information
```

Please start collecting your materials for the August Sales Conference
slides and have them in my office ASAP but no later than Wednesday, July 12.

What to Send Me

We will probably use the same style as last year, so I need:

1. Jacket cover

2. Photo of author
        Exceptions: no photo
                     unusable photo
                     no sense in showing author's face
                     multiple authors with no group photo

OPTIONAL: Provide only if they truly support presentation. We want to keep
material at a minimum for good flow.

3. Competing titles

4. Previous successful books (with sales figures!)

5. Press clippings of note, quotes, etc.

OTHER INFORMATION: Anything that needs to be read thoroughly should be
included in the accompanying brochure, not used for a slide.

If you have any questions, please call me. Thanks!

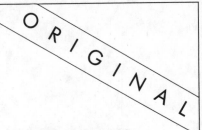

To: John Mittleman   Date: September 2, 1997

From: Sally Schwartz   cc: Distribution

Subject: Expanded ZIP Code Seminar

On August 29, 1997, Sally Schwartz attended the Golden Gate District Postal Customer Council Luncheon Seminar in San Francisco with her guest, Howard Bricker. The high interest in the Expanded ZIP Code was evident by the large number who attended.

Tom Bohan and Jerry Dewey of the Expanded ZIP Code Task Force, Washington, D.C., were the speakers. The following is a synopsis of their messages pertinent to SPECTOR.

1. The USPS places a high value on the local PCC activities and is glad to lend support and assistance to PCC activities.

2. The benefits of the 11-digit ZIP Code were reviewed:

    A. Able to use more sophisticated mechanization and automation
    B. Reducing errors
    C. Improving cost effectiveness
    D. Increasing efficiency level

3. The USPS will announce in October 1997 the incentive programs they will have for the businesses that use the 11-digit ZIP. There is definite indication that these programs will be the type that can benefit SPECTOR.

4. Businesses will be informed of their Expanded ZIP Code numbers December 1997. At that time Computer Tapes will be available for companies concerned with address labels. The tapes will be on loan for several weeks for approx. $25.

5. Handwritten mail should also use 11-digit Zip. The OCR can read some of them and the rest can be sorted faster when the USPS rekeys their semiautomatic sorting units.

6. The Bar Code currently on our Business Reply Envelopes and Cards will not need to be altered.

7. The USPS processed 104 billion pieces of mail and 80% of it was generated by businesses. If businesses use the 11-digit ZIP, the desired benefits can take place.

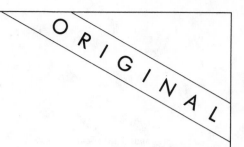

8. When more than one ZIP is assigned to a business in one location, the Post Office will not be fine-sorting into each ZIP. Possibly they will in the future.

9. We need to examine our stock of window envelopes to make sure they are the proper size to accommodate the Expanded ZIP.

10. When addressing an envelope, a space in the bottom right side of the envelope must be left for the Bar Code.

11. All of our stationery needs to be examined and reprinted with the Expanded ZIP, including business cards and advertising material.

12. Among the other benefits arising from attending the Postal Forum West, it will be a must this December because of the Expanded Zip Code information that will be available. Registration information will definitely arrive in September.

13. The USPS is still developing ways to help businesses to adjust to the 11-digit ZIP. They are encouraging setting up meetings within the company and the Customer Service Rep will help by speaking at the meeting or arranging for someone in the USPS with the needed information to speak.

14. The proper addressing format was emphasized and it will be necessary to include this in the Company Practice and the Reference Guide.

15. One of the first steps the USPS recommends when we receive our Expanded ZIP Code is to print it on our Business Reply envelopes and cards for the initial education of our public.

16. The 11-digit ZIP use is aimed at the letter because it is machinable. Use the Expanded ZIP on the flats also because it will help with the sorting.

There is no need to "panic" because of implementation of the Expanded ZIP Code. The USPS appears to have a realistic view of the problems that will arise. The long range benefit to Spector is evident in the future postage savings. Meanwhile we have 3 years to make the necessary changes and educate employees and customers.

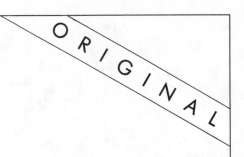

DISTRIBUTION—MAIL DATA

All mail stops—Park City/Saint Joseph County (H23)
All U.S. sales offices

Chairman of the Board
    L. Mayer (2810)

President
    I. Thalberg (2847)

Group Presidents
    G. Stone (2213)
    M. Milton (1453)
    P. Fortune (2922)
    H. Hunt (1890)
    J. Pizotto (1148)

Division Managers
    B. Ivaldi (3241)
    J. Iturbi (2158)
    G. Brandiwine (3188)
    S. Lipman (2001)
    P. Summers (2890)
    L. Tavernetti (1297)
    V. Satata (2255)
    S. Sirandelli (3528)
    C. Charles (3208)
    E. Wichynski (8320)
    K. Hedargyn (3985)

Corporate Finance
    H. Hurst (3928)
    D. Vanent (5927)
    D. Carpenter (2194)
    W. Esposito (3045)
    J. Walsh (9723)
    C. Vendal (1938)
    S. Sylvester (8720)
    B. Lupien (2834)
    B. Gorman (5436)
    W. Walker (8528)
    A. Albani (8635)
    M. Ralliman (9247)

Division Controllers
    F. Butterworth (5935)
    B. Caliban (4685)
    G. Weymouth (9675)
    S. Millay (3624)
    J. La Rue (8935)
    S. Epstein (8985)
    D. LaBounty (3764)
    C. Chin (5320)
    J. Holt (8982)
    Y. Nakemura (5373)
    B. O'Shaughnessy (4698)
    D. Gish (3437)
    S. Greenstreet (5434)
    R. Paige (9898)

Marketing Managers
    L. Taterdine (3456)
    K. Stookey (3720)
    B. Rhee (4328)
    N. Sparks (2393)
    J. Coogan (6725)
    J. Cocchi (4384)
    D. Kellogg (2592)
    F. Falco (7344)
    V. Fink (8446)
    S. Selwyn (2350)
    H. Hammersmith (2842)
    U. Undiru (9374)
    K. Kaplan (7682)
    G. George (5340)

Advertising Staff
    S. Sinclair (8572)
    L. Wong (4340)
    L. Lincoln (6524)
    I. Court (8326)
    S. Boswell (5972)

Group Controllers
    F. Malinari (3597)
    H. Hallinan (5934)
    F. Cutting (6983)
    V. Oldier (5297)
    R. Ponselle (8267)
    S. Dubin (4963)
    M. Cocelli (7253)
    B. Jensen (6463)

Division Controllers
    O. Besmith (8524)
    F. Floyd (9273)
    C. Graver (8664)

Purchasing Managers
    S. Gaymont (2346)
    A. Allwyn (8752)
    B. Loyon (9380)
    C. Danforth (4285)
    E. Dugan (3672)
    G. Wilmot (2592)
    C. Gambler (8376)
    W. Van Dyke (4562)
    D. Risdon (9328)
    D. Koll (9845)
    M. Johnson (9623)
    R. Walsetech (5244)
    M. Fauvel (7392)
    F. Granger (5643)
    J. Hughes (6857)

ADDITIONAL DISTRIBUTION

    A. Rutledge (7495)
    C. Baretti (8320)
    S. Beasley (8576)
    C. Chang (3928)
    B. Finger (5947)
    N. Franlyn (8235)
    Y. Yahoudi (6958)
    V. Gassman (3575)
    S. Winters (9423)
    S. Shigito (8575)
    E. Ellyott (6530)
    S. Fabriel (5184)
    T. McCoy (2430)
    J. Beethoven (8560)
    J. Stein (1538)
    J. MacDonald (4298)
    J. Ralph (6134)
    J. Hailey (9891)

    S. Dolittle (3554)
    R. Schippers (2384)
    R. Valentino (6235)
    W. Hearst (9546)
    V. Sadoti (3162)
    T. Coster (5423)
    E. Houstley (8240)
    R. Barthelmess (3156)
    M. Schink (2482)
    P. Foscotti (9432)
    J. Katz (1843)
    P. Wong (5620)
    L. Lipschitz (2310)
    D. Dranke (4152)
    M. Tass (3694)
    E. Tessman (2438)
    S. Wittle (5111)
    M. Espinoza (3424)

    G. Subhashi (9361)
    A. Peasdale (3524)
    E. Enderson (8524)
    W. Hickock (3926)
    T. Whipple (5183)
    T. Dugan (4250)
    S. Travey (2384)
    R. Ramanaya (1365)
    R. Dooley (4266)
    S. Silverado (3195)
    D. Zanuck (2832)
    R. Novarro (4160)
    M. Douris (5483)
    L. Youngh (9132)
    K. Wonderly (5483)
    N. Beatty (9632)
    M. March (1894)
    H. Knowles (3213)

WHAT TO DO

Don't confuse memos and minutes. This writer has transcribed her notes from the seminar and sent them. Did this writer's 143 readers need to know everything she has told them? Remember, this is a disguise of a *real* memo!

If each of those 143 people takes only three minutes to read the memo, plus another two minutes to handle and file it, imagine the cost to the company. Assume that top management cost the firm a hundred dollars an hour, that middle management cost fifty dollars an hour, and the department heads only twenty-five dollars an hour. What did reading this memo cost Spector? (Probably about $5,200.) Was it worth it?

MINUTES are for: details,

reportage,

record keeping

MEMOS are for: conclusions,

requests,

decisions

1. Put a check next to every item that describes an action Spector needs to take because of the new expanded zip code.

2. Put a star next to *actual* benefits to Spector (not the post office).

3. Circle anything that tells how the reader can get more information about expanded zip codes.

ANSWERS

1. Actions that Spector needs to take because of the new zip code are described in items five, nine, eleven, fourteen, and fifteen. They are summarized in the rewrite under "Changes Spector Needs to Make."

2. *Actual* benefits to Spector (not to the post office) are not yet clear, except for the minor item of computer tapes described in item four. They are referred to under "Benefits to Spector."

3. More information can be obtained by:
   a. attending the December meeting (stated in item twelve).
   b. reading the minutes of the meeting (we have added this).

• • • •

OUR REWRITE

SUBJECT CHANGED FROM Expanded ZIP Code Seminar

TO Impact of Expanded Zip Code on SPECTOR

UNNECESSARY INFORMATION: The original contains much information useful to specific departments (such as leaving space on envelopes), but not important to the chairman of the board.

A BETTER WAY: Obviously Spector needs to prepare for the coming change. This writer might have asked her supervisor about preparing a brief article for the company in-house newsletter on the subject.

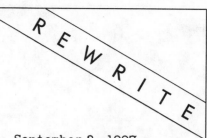

TO: John Mittleman   DATE: September 2, 1997

FROM: Sally Schwartz   CC: Distribution

SUBJECT: Impact of Expanded Zip Code on SPECTOR

FOR: [ ] action   [ ] decision   [X] information

The United States Postal Service will begin using an expanded 11-digit Zip Code, beginning in December. SPECTOR will have three years to convert to this new system, but we should begin planning now.

CHANGES SPECTOR NEEDS TO MAKE

Stationery: All of our stationery needs to be reprinted with the expanded Zip, including business cards and advertising material.

Company Practice and Reference Guide will need to be updated.

Personnel Education: Employees and customers will need to learn new procedures.

BENEFITS TO SPECTOR

The USPS will announce incentive programs in October. These will include computer tapes for address labels.

MORE INFORMATION

December Informational Meeting: I recommend that affected departments send a representative to Postal Service's major informational meeting in December. Registration information will arrive in September.

Detailed minutes of the August 29 USPS informational meeting are available in the Shipping Department and will be sent to you on request.

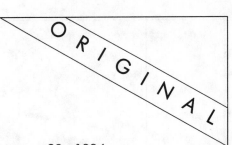

TO: J. Baer   DATE: February 29, 1994

FROM: W. Crane   CC: C. Katz
                                 J. Asch
                                 P. Doag

SUBJECT: Equipment Inspection

1) <u>Hardware—Green & Wood Associates</u>
    We are advised by Mr. Peter Updike, Green & Wood, that the first unit
    completion will be around March 18 or 19, 1994. We therefore are
    planning to fly west March 18 with Mr. Updike in order to visit the Green
    & Wood plant on March 19.

2) <u>Power System—Haroldsen Company</u>
    Mr. Jim Lewis, Haroldsen, advises us that the prototype P/S will be
    available for inspection at their Los Angeles plant about March 18,
    1994. My plan is to fly from Green & Wood down to Los Angeles the
    afternoon or early evening of March 20, and visit the Haroldsen
    facility March 21, returning that same evening.

3) <u>Disc Units—Germany</u>
    Wolffenbach, Inc. advises that the first (prototype) disc unit will be
    ready for inspection March 29, 1994, provided they receive the
    prototype Datarex disc unit by March 25, 1994. In this regard, Datarex
    advises that the prototype disc unit will be ready to ship March 14 or
    18, 1994. Please arrange for it to be sent via air freight directly to
    Germany (Hamburg) for delivery to Wolffenbach's plant in Stocken. We
    intend to be in Germany to inspect this unit on April 19.

    Meisterwerks AGI advises that the prototype disc unit will be available
    for inspection on or about April 5 or 6. Datarex is shipping, along with
    the prototype unit for Wolffenbach, a template for the proper location
    of the mounting holes and two complete sets of stainless steel mounting
    bolts, lock nuts and washers (27 each set). Please advise our Spector
    personnel in Germany who will receive the disc unit, template, etc., to
    separate the unit and one set of bolts, nuts, and washers, and send them
    to Wolffenbach, Stocken, and to send the template and other set of
    bolts, nuts, and washers to Meisterwerks, Hamburg. Also please arrange
    to send one of our spare TK 80—944 J S09Q (blue) Datarex units to Germany
    for installation into the Meisterwerks unit. This unit should be in
    their hands on or before April 1st.

WHAT TO DO

Sometimes writers try to be "efficient" and turn memos into mini-newsletters. Distinctly separate subjects deserve separate memos, if only for convenience in filing. (Would you recall a year from now that details about a sales contract are in a memo headed "Fire Prevention"?)

At first glance, this real memo looks very well organized.

1. What is the subject of this memo? Is there more than one subject?

2. Would this information be clearer if it were divided into two separate memos?

3. Would a chart make any of this information easier to understand?

4. If so, what information would you present in the form of a chart? Indicate the headings below.

ORIGINAL

TO: J. Baer   DATE: February 29, 1994

FROM: W. Crane   CC: C. Katz
J. Asch
P. Doag

SUBJECT: Equipment Inspection

1) Hardware—Green & Wood Associates
We are advised by Mr. Peter Updike, Green & Wood, that the first unit
completion will be around March 18 or 19, 1994. We therefore are
planning to fly west March 18 with Mr. Updike in order to visit the Green
& Wood plant on March 19.

2) Power System—Haroldsen Company
Mr. Jim Lewis, Haroldsen, advises us that the prototype P/S will be
available for inspection at their Los Angeles plant about March 18,
1994. My plan is to fly from Green & Wood down to Los Angeles the
afternoon or early evening of March 20, and visit the Haroldsen
facility March 21, returning that same evening.

3) Disc Units—Germany
Wolffenbach, Inc. advises that the first (prototype) disc unit will be
ready for inspection March 29, 1994, provided they receive the
prototype Datarex disc unit by March 25, 1994. In this regard, Datarex
advises that the prototype disc unit will be ready to ship March 14 or
18, 1994. Please arrange for it to be sent via air freight directly to
Germany (Hamburg) for delivery to Wolffenbach's plant in Stocken. We
intend to be in Germany to inspect this unit on April 19.

Meisterwerks AGI advises that the prototype disc unit will be available
for inspection on or about April 5 or 6. Datarex is shipping, along with
the prototype unit for Wolffenbach, a template for the proper location
of the mounting holes and two complete sets of stainless steel mounting
bolts, lock nuts and washers (27 each set). Please advise our Spector
personnel in Germany who will receive the disc unit, template, etc., to
separate the unit and one set of bolts, nuts, and washers, and send them
to Wolffenbach, Stocken, and to send the template and other set of
bolts, nuts, and washers to Meisterwerks, Hamburg. Also please arrange
to send one of our spare TK 80-944 J S09Q (blue) Datarex units to Germany
for installation into the Meisterwerks unit. This unit should be in
their hands on or before April 1st.

WHAT WE DID

ANSWERS

1. The subjects of the memo are:
    Datarex Shipping Instructions
    My Inspection Schedule

2. Yes, this information would be clearer if it were divided into two separate memos.

3. Yes, a chart would clarify the inspection schedule.

4. See our Rewrite B for possible headings.

• • • •

OUR REWRITES

We have divided this memo into two, since the original expands to two pages when appropriate headings and a chart are added. It's interesting that the first point of the memo—the shipping instructions—are not mentioned in the original subject title: ''Equipment Inspection.''

Rewrite A is opposite. Turn the page to see Rewrite B.

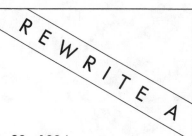

TO: J. Baer   DATE: February 29, 1994

FROM: W. Crane   CC: C. Katz
                                  J. Asch
                                  P. Doag

SUBJECT: Datarex Shipping Instructions

FOR: [X] action   [ ] decision   [ ] information

Please arrange the following:

1. Airfreight a Datarex shipment to Wolffenbach's plant in Stocken as soon as it is ready. The shipment will contain a prototype disc unit, a template for locating mounting holes, and two sets of mounting bolts, lock nuts, and washers (27 each set).

    <u>To ship between March 14 and March 18.</u>

2. Instruct our Spector Receiving personnel at Hamburg to separate the shipment into two lots and reship it:

    Lot 1: Reship template and one set of bolts, nuts, and washers to Meisterwerks AGI's plant in Frankfurt for use in Meisterwerks AGI's prototype disc unit.

            <u>Must arrive by [date].</u>

    Lot 2: Reship the Datarex disc unit and the second set of bolts, nuts, and washers to Wolffenbach's plant in Stocken, Germany.

            <u>Must arrive by March 25.</u>

3. Send one of our spare TK 80-944 J S09Q (blue) Datarex units to Meisterwerks' plant at Frankfurt for installation in their prototype disc unit.

        <u>Must arrive by April 1.</u>

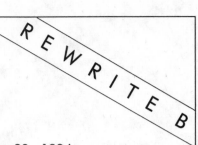

TO: J. Baer   DATE: February 29, 1994

FROM: W. Crane   CC: C. Katz
                                  J. Asch
                                  P. Doag

SUBJECT: My Inspection Schedule

FOR: [ ] action   [ ] decision   [X] information

Item	Producer	Completion Date	Inspection Date/Location
Hardware	Green & Wood	March 18–19	March 19 G&W plant * [address]
Power System	Haroldsen	March 18	March 21 Haroldsen plant, Los Angeles *
Disc Unit	Wolffenbach	March 29	April 19 Stocken, Germany
Disc Unit	Meisterwerks	April 5–6	No inspection date set Hamburg, Germany **

*I will leave March 18, return the evening of March 21.
**I will be in Germany for the Wolffenbach inspection on April 19.

DON'T BE BRER RABBIT

When you don't find the purpose up front in a business communication, imagine that the author is muttering and doodling in front of you before talking directly to you.

Think: "Here we go again with once-upon-a-time." Then skip over the disorganized preamble.

If you remember the story of Brer Rabbit and the Tar Baby, think of memos without a purpose up front as "Tar Babies" and avoid getting stuck. Don't let a bad writer take you the long way round the block. Start reading where the purpose begins, find what you need to know, read it wherever it is, and dump the rest.

CHAPTER 2

Purpose Up Front

 Why are you writing? Do you need action? A decision? Are you giving information? What is the most important thing you are saying?

Put the most important thing in the first sentence or paragraph. Put any conclusions or recommendations at the beginning, not at the end.

Let your reader know immediately why you are writing:

> I need your action.
> I need your decision.
> Here is information.

For memos, establish a company-wide system of boxes that the writer can check off.

```
For:  [ ] action  [ ] decision  [ ] information
```

This lets readers know immediately why they are reading and alerts them to requests for action and decisions. (It also helps writers clarify their own purpose for writing.)

TO: Distribution   DATE: September 26, 1994

FROM: Jack Healy

SUBJECT: Material Receiving

Approximately one month ago, Spector initiated its own receiving department. This effort was undertaken to eliminate many of the problems that had occurred during the time that Spector utilized the existing building receiving department. This has been successfully accomplished.

Unfortunately, the receiving area can operate efficiently only if all products received by the company are routed through the receiving area. This is not happening in all cases. In particular the hand carrying of product into Spector tends to bypass the receiving and incoming inspection procedures.

In an effort to eliminate this problem, it is being requested that effective 9/26/94, all materials hand carried into the company and acquired through a purchase order, regardless of whether it is a specific or blanket purchase order, be delivered to Tod Wilkes, our receiving clerk, so that the proper paperwork can be completed and incoming inspection be performed if necessary. Normal receiving turn-around time will be 24 hours, with critical need items being processed within one hour of receipt. With these time commitments, there is absolutely no reason why any material ordered under the above conditions should bypass the receiving functions.

Furthermore, it is requested that all departments in receipt of material that has managed to bypass the receiving function submit a list of all such material, such lists noting the purchase order number, date of receipt at Spector, the quantity received, the vendor, and the current location of all material, to the I.C. department no later than 9/30/94. Such material may be subject to recall by the I.C. department until such time as it is determined that these products meet our incoming inspection requirements.

It is mandatory that the above procedures be followed in every case of receipt of hand carried merchandise. Only in this manner can we insure that proper accounting and incoming inspection records are maintained on such materials. Your cooperation is expected in this matter.

Regards,

Jack Healy

WHAT TO DO

Here is another classic once-upon-a-time. Skip through it until you find the purpose.

Telling people something they don't want to hear is never easy. This writer tried to soften the news by giving a history of the situation. Do you think it helped?

1. What is the "news"—the purpose—of this memo? Underline the sentence(s) that tell you what the writer wants.

2. Is there any other information that should be highlighted?

3. How does the tone of the first paragraph differ from the tone of the last paragraph?

4. Look at the fourth paragraph. Can you think of a way to organize that information better? Rewrite the fourth paragraph here.

Wʜᴀᴛ ᴡᴇ ᴅɪᴅ

TO: Distribution   DATE: September 26, 1994

FROM: Jack Healy

SUBJECT: Material Receiving

Approximately one month ago, Spector initiated its own receiving department. This effort was undertaken to eliminate many of the problems that had occurred during the time that Spector utilized the existing building receiving department. This has been successfully accomplished.

Unfortunately, the receiving area can operate efficiently only if all products received by the company are routed through the receiving area. This is not happening in all cases. In particular the hand carrying of product into Spector tends to bypass the receiving and incoming inspection procedures.

In an effort to eliminate this problem, it is being requested that effective 9/26/94, all materials hand carried into the company and acquired through a purchase order, regardless of whether it is a specific or blanket purchase order, be delivered to Tod Wilkes, our receiving clerk, so that the proper paperwork can be completed and incoming inspection be performed if necessary. Normal receiving turn-around time will be 24 hours, with critical need items being processed within one hour of receipt. With these time commitments, there is absolutely no reason why any material ordered under the above conditions should bypass the receiving functions.

Furthermore, it is requested that all departments in receipt of material that has managed to bypass the receiving function submit a list of all such material, such lists noting the purchase order number, date of receipt at Spector, the quantity received, the vendor, and the current location of all material, to the I.C. department no later than 9/30/94. Such material may be subject to recall by the I.C. department until such time as it is determined that these products meet our incoming inspection requirements.

It is mandatory that the above procedures be followed in every case of receipt of hand carried merchandise. Only in this manner can we insure that proper accounting and incoming inspection records are maintained on such materials. Your cooperation is expected in this matter.

Regards,

Jack Healy

ANSWERS

1. The purposes are found in paragraph three—"effective 9/26/94, all materials hand carried into the company and acquired through a purchase order . . . be delivered to Tod Wilkes" and paragraph four—"all departments . . . submit a list of all such material."

2. Highlight response dates. Also, listing the needed information makes it easier to respond. The writer could also have prepared and attached a simple reply form.

3. First paragraph: chatty. Last paragraph: dictatorial.

4. The information in the fourth paragraph of the original appears in paragraph two of the rewrite as a list.

•   •   •   •   •

OUR REWRITE

TONE: In an effort to justify an unpopular directive, this writer has "softened" his instructions into four paragraphs of convoluted English. Then he suddenly reverts to strong "officialese," possibly because he recalls that a previous directive wasn't obeyed. (Perhaps his previous directive was just as hard for the readers to understand.)

HEADINGS: We have changed the two instructions into headings, used clear, concise, action sentences, dropped all the background information and justifications. Either the writer has the authority to request the procedure or he doesn't. Respect for the reader can't hurt his cause.

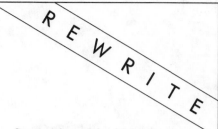

TO: Distribution   DATE: September 26, 1994

FROM: Jack Healy

SUBJECT: Change in Receiving Procedures

FOR: [X] action   [ ] decision   [ ] information

We must have your help so we can maintain proper accounting and inspection records.

1. <u>Starting today, deliver all hand–carried materials</u> acquired through a purchase order to Tod Wilkes, receiving clerk, in our new Receiving Department. No exceptions!

   Normal turnaround time will be 24 hours. Critically needed items will be processed within one hour.

2. <u>Submit a list by Friday,</u> September 30, to Inventory Control of all material that has not passed through our own Receiving Department since it began operations on August 15. We need the following information for accounting and inventory control:

   a. P.O. number
   b. date received
   c. vendor
   d. quantity received
   e. current location of this material

   Some of these items may need to be recalled by Inventory Control so that we can be sure they meet our inspection quality standards.

ORIGINAL

TO: T.L. Philips, DR 467   DATE: May 15, 1996

SUBJECT: FOCUS PROJECT HEAD COUNT STATUS   CC: Ralph Bowers

In line with our discussions with Ralph Bowers this date, I have reviewed the current FOCUS organization and near term manpower forecast, and compared same against the 1996 budget prepared last year.

Since the budget was cast, we have incurred a significant increase in client oriented information and coordination requests, and have further expanded and developed our program for controlling Davis consulting research costs. In accordance with these needs, we have added two individuals to the CR liaison staff to provide increased capability to direct and measure Davis operations and to assure achieving maximum economies in the Davis research effort. Furthermore, we have utilized these liaison positions together with existing positions in Chicago to develop a new program and task force operation aimed at installing and administering the use of a national computerized central information system. I forecast that this effort will be required into late 1997, which of course, means that our staffing of the liaison office in Cleveland including the existing liaison manager would be retained at the level of three individuals throughout that period of time. This time period is consistent with the anticipated completion by Davis of all the basic units in FOCUS's consumer resource center, and should take us well into the middle stage of the mini-research stations in rural areas.

In line with increasing requests by Concerned Consumers management for additional dedicated interface support into the New York City office, we have established the position of Concerned Consumers project manager and have assigned J.E. Randolph to that position. This has allowed us to expand our interface with Concerned Consumers to a substantial degree and satisfy client demands in this area. This, together with the additional staffing of the liaison office and establishment of the computer telecommunications system, has allowed me to personally devote more time to management oriented areas, such as Davis administration and cost control, Concerned Consumers legal matters, and overall oriented activities.

The preceding is intended to provide you with general background and basis as to why the current FOCUS staff head count forecast of 20 for the year 1997 is three higher than the 17 individuals projected by the 1997 budget. Currently 8 of these positions have been filled. One position is now in posting, and an approved requisition and position guide developed for the final position. This latter position will be filled in approximately two weeks upon the return of J.T. Cooper to his permanent assignment as Manager of FOCUS Project Administration. Currently Mr. Cooper is functioning both in that position and as acting manager of the Davis liaison office until R.M. Roth has been adequately trained to completely handle the liaison position.

Please advise if there is any further information you require.

Robert B. Sandwell, Manager

WHAT TO DO

Does this writer sound sure of the reasons for his decision to add three employees? Does he impress you with the clarity of his thinking? Does he sound confident of the reader's approval? What if the reader has never met the writer and must judge him and his abilities by this memo?

This memo is written the way that most of us think. Don't despair if your first drafts look like this. That's perfectly okay. Just don't send them until you have crafted them for the *convenience of the reader*.

1. Scan this memo to find its purpose.

    Does it request action?
    Does it ask for a decision?
    Does it supply information?

2. Underline the purpose.

3. Make a check next to each sentence that actually says something pertinent to the purpose.

4. Pretend you are a newspaper reporter. Write a headline below that announces the major news in this memo.

TO: T.L. Philips, DR 467   DATE: May 15, 1996
SUBJECT: FOCUS PROJECT HEAD COUNT STATUS   CC: Ralph Bowers

In line with our discussions with Ralph Bowers this date, I have reviewed the current FOCUS organization and near term manpower forecast, and compared same against the 1996 budget prepared last year.

Since the budget was cast, we have incurred a significant increase in client oriented information and coordination requests, and have further expanded and developed our program for controlling Davis consulting research costs. In accordance with these needs, we have added two individuals to the CR liaison staff to provide increased capability to direct and measure Davis operations and to assure achieving maximum economies in the Davis research effort. Furthermore, we have utilized these liaison positions together with existing positions in Chicago to develop a new program and task force operation aimed at installing and administering the use of a national computerized central information system. I forecast that this effort will be required into late 1997, which of course, means that our staffing of the liaison office in Cleveland including the existing liaison manager would be retained at the level of three individuals throughout that period of time. This time period is consistent with the anticipated completion by Davis of all the basic units in FOCUS's consumer resource center, and should take us well into the middle stage of the mini-research stations in rural areas.

In line with increasing requests by Concerned Consumers management for additional dedicated interface support into the New York City office, we have established the position of Concerned Consumers project manager and have assigned J.E. Randolph to that position. This has allowed us to expand our interface with Concerned Consumers to a substantial degree and satisfy client demands in this area. This, together with the additional staffing of the liaison office and establishment of the computer telecommunications system, has allowed me to personally devote more time to management oriented areas, such as Davis administration and cost control, Concerned Consumers legal matters, and overall oriented activities.

The preceding is intended to provide you with general background and basis as to why the current FOCUS staff head count forecast of 20 for the year 1997 is three higher than the 17 individuals projected by the 1997 budget. Currently 8 of these positions have been filled. One position is now in posting, and an approved requisition and position guide developed for the final position. This latter position will be filled in approximately two weeks upon the return of J.T. Cooper to his permanent assignment as Manager of FOCUS Project Administration. Currently Mr. Cooper is functioning both in that position and as acting manager of the Davis liaison office until R.W. Roth has been adequately trained to completely handle the liaison position.

Please advise if there is any further information you require.

Robert B. Sandwell, Manager

ANSWERS

1. Does it request action?
    Does it ask for a decision?*
    Does it supply information?
    * (Because the writer offers so many supports for his own decision, there is also the implication that he may be hoping for the reader's approval—a decision on the part of the reader.)

2. The purpose or main point of this memo—that the FOCUS Project has three employees too many—is in the fourth paragraph.

3. The supports of the main point appear in our rewrite under the heading "Background." Documentation of the increased work load is moved to an attachment.

4. An appropriate subject headline would be:

    Three Unbudgeted FOCUS Personnel

• • • •

OUR REWRITE

SUBJECT CHANGED FROM   FOCUS Project Head Count Status

TO   Three Unbudgeted FOCUS Personnel

CONTENT: When you wade through all that verbiage, the decision appears to be a sound one, but few readers would have the time or patience to figure that out.

ATTACHMENT   listed.

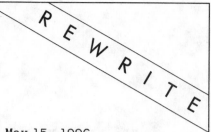

TO: T. L. Philips   DATE: May 15, 1996

FROM: R. P. Sandwell   CC: Ralph Bowers

SUBJECT: Three Unbudgeted FOCUS Personnel

FOR: [ ] action   [ ] decision   [X] information

We now have three more employees on the FOCUS Project than are provided for in the budget—20 actual versus 17 budgeted.

The three additional employees will be needed through late next year and I anticipate that additional personnel costs will be more than offset by the cost savings they will generate.

Background

We have added two positions to the Consulting Research liaison staff to monitor Davis in order to minimize research costs. See attachment for justification. We anticipate keeping these two extra positions to install and administer the use of a national computerized central information system until the system is self-operative in late 1997. One of the two positions is already filled and the other is posted.

The third position is an additional staff liaison to deal with Concerned Consumers in New York City so that I can be free to manage the overall project. We've assigned J. E. Randolph as Concerned Consumers project manager.

Att: Increased Client Research Requests

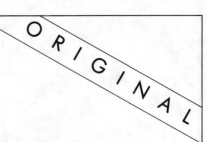

TO: Dave Matthews   DATE: June 16, 1994

SUBJECT: Smoke Detection Equipment   FROM: Joanne Davis

I am enclosing some correspondence dated October 29, 1993, from Smithson, Inc., as well as a letter dated November 14, 1993, from Allied Insurance on the subject of smoke detection equipment at the Dallas office.

Effective April 15, 1994, we were advised by Smithson that an additional annual premium of $26,500 would be charged to your office to cover the cost of reinsurance due to inadequate fire protection. Cost to provide smoke detectors at your office was previously estimated in the neighborhood of $64,000. If this is in fact true, then it appears we could commit the capital expenditure and still obtain a return on investment.

What we would propose at this point is to determine:

1) whether or not any changes have been made in the layout of your office, staff size, or other protection considerations since Smithson's last visit in Fall of 1993.

2) firm up final cost indications on provision of smoke detectors in accordance with specifications provided by Smithson and approved by Allied.

We would appreciate your thoughts on Item 1) for now.

cc: J. Roberts, Smithson
     F. Crane
     T. Baer
     K. Katz
     R. Ruester
     C. Wong
     J. Toki

WHAT TO DO

Does the writer want a decision? Or a survey? Or both?

1. Underline the sentence(s) that indicate he wants a decision.

2. Underline the sentence(s) that indicate he wants a survey.

3. Write a new first sentence that begins with: "Do you want . . ."

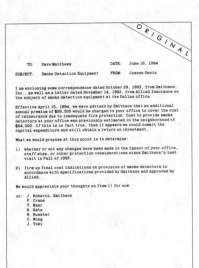

ANSWERS

1. The two sentences that indicate he may want a decision are in paragraph three: "What we would propose at this point is to determine . . ." and paragraph four: "We would appreciate your thoughts on Item 1) for now."

2. The sentence that indicates he wants a survey is in paragraph three: "1) whether or not any changes have been made in the layout of your office, staff size, or other protection considerations since Smithson's last visit in Fall of 1993."

3. See the new first sentences in the two rewrites.

•   •   •   •

OUR REWRITE

We have crafted two different versions of this memo, one asking for a decision and one asking for action (taking a survey). Rewrite A is opposite. Turn the page to see Rewrite B.

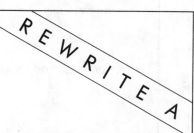

This version is crafted to ask for a decision.

TO: Dave Matthews   DATE: June 16, 1994

FROM: Joanne Davis   CC: J. Roberts, Smithson
                                          F. Crane
                                          T. Baer
                                          K. Katz
                                          R. Ruester
                                          C. Wong
                                          J. Toki

SUBJECT: Cost Savings of Smoke Detectors

FOR: [ ] action   [X] decision   [ ] information

Do you want to pay $64,000 to install smoke detectors or do you want to pay
an additional annual fire insurance premium of $26,500 for not having them?

You will want to consider:

1. Whether you have made any changes in office layout since Smithson's
    visit in the fall of 1993 that may affect our insurance rate.

2. Whether $64,000 is still an accurate figure for the cost of
    installing smoke detectors.

Att: Smithson letter, 10/29/93
      Allied Insurance letter, 11/14/93

This version is crafted to ask for a survey.

REWRITE B

TO: Dave Matthews   DATE: June 16, 1994

FROM: Joanne Davis   CC: J. Roberts, Smithson
                                        F. Crane
                                        T. Baer
                                        K. Katz
                                        R. Ruester
                                        C. Wong
                                        J. Toki

SUBJECT: Increased Insurance Rate
            Due to Lack of Smoke Detectors

    FOR: [X] action   [ ] decision   [ ] information

Have you made any changes in office layout or storage areas since Smithson made an inspection last fall? They are charging your office an additional $26,500 due to inadequate fire protection.

Please get a current estimate for smoke detection equipment installation. If last year's quote of $64,000 is still good, we could commit the capital expenditure.

Att: Smithson letter, 10/29/93
     Allied Insurance letter, 11/14/93

CHAPTER 3

Conclusion Up Front

 Put your conclusion, recommendation, summary, or abstract first. What are you recommending? Why?

"Conclusion" means *end*, but don't let that fool you. In business, the bottom line comes first, both philosophically and in written communications.

Put your punch line first. Then list your supports:

> background information
> statistics
> legal or financial considerations
> . . . etc.

They're there if the reader needs them, but they don't obscure your conclusion, recommendation, or summary.

TO: Molly Yeckley   DATE: January 23, 1998

FROM: Joe Marchi   SUBJECT: Shipments

Shipment status for the month of January 1998.

According to the originally scheduled unit volume forecasted for shipment, we have received 51% into Sales Stock, as of this date (1/23/98).

This leaves us both with 49% left to ship in the limited time remaining.

There is 16% available straight—time labor left before cutoff on Friday, 1/26, at 9:00 AM, and 26% of our available straight—time labor left before month—end.

We will make every effort possible to maximize the highest level of shipments for the month, that is humanly rational, by working overtime during the week and on Saturday, 1/27/98.

The highest concentrated effort will be on products that arrive before cutoff and on completing Denver orders.

Other units will be packed on a "best—effort" basis, as time allows.

The projected probability of meeting the desired shipment forecast for January 1998 is: <u>POOR</u>.

WHAT TO DO

1. Where is the "news" in this memo? Find it and underline it.

2. Put a check next to each of the "supports"—proofs, examples, causes—for the writer's conclusion.

3. Draw a circle around any information that is left. How would you categorize this other information?

4. Create a heading for each category of information and write them below.

ANSWERS

1. The "news" is the conclusion: "The projected probability of meeting the desired shipment forecast for January 1998 is: *POOR*." Put the news first.

2. Supports: Forty-nine percent of the month's orders must be shipped, but only 26 percent of the allocated man-hours remain (16 percent before some arbitrary cutoff date).

3. Other information: The writer describes his efforts to lessen the problem, his *solution*.

4. Possible headings: Overtime Planned
   Priorities

• • • •

OUR REWRITE

**SUBJECT
CHANGED FROM** Shipments
    TO January XYZ Shipments Behind
    Schedule
    "Shipments" is a generic title.
    What shipments? What about
    them? Be specific! (But try not
    to use more than eight words—
    subjects shouldn't be detailed
    paragraphs.)

CHART compares the percentage of work remaining to the percentage of man-hours available.

HEADINGS: The headings "Overtime Planned" and "Priorities" alert the reader to the writer's proposed solutions.

TO: Molly Yeckley   DATE: January 23, 1998

FROM: Joe Marchi

SUBJECT: January XYZ Shipments Behind Schedule

FOR: [ ] action   [ ] decision   [X] information

The probability of meeting our desired XYZ shipment forecast for January is <u>POOR</u>.

As of January 23:

    49% of shipments remain to be done, BUT:

    16% of our available straight-time labor remains before cutoff on Friday, 1/26, at 9:00 A.M.

    26% of our available straight-time labor remains before month-end.

<u>Overtime Planned</u>

We will make every rational and possible effort to meet the schedule by working overtime during the week and on Saturday, 1/27/98.

<u>Priorities</u>

The highest concentrated effort will be on products that arrive before cutoff and on completing Denver orders. Other units will be packed on a "best-effort" basis as time allows.

SAVE TIME AND MONEY, ASK YOURSELF

- Would a phone call take care of this matter more efficiently?
  If so, would it have to be documented?
- Does the reader know immediately why he is reading?
- Does the reader know who is being asked to do what?
  And when?
- Have I summarized the essentials on one page?
- Have I minimized the list of recipients?
- Have I enclosed/attached the materials referred to and listed them at the bottom?
- Have I used simple, declarative sentences?
- Should I consult a company attorney before sending this?

CHAPTER 4

Headings

 Can readers find out what they want to know quickly? Is your information organized into logical sections for the convenience of your reader?

Headings are actually the "subheads" that you use throughout your text to alert the reader whenever you change subjects.

Good headings have two uses:

1. They let the reader scan your communication, seeing with a quick glance what you are saying. They provide an overview.

2. They help you to group the information in your exploratory writing into logical categories, such as:

    -   what each department or person is expected to do
    -   alternative actions (choose one)
    -   a series of supports for a conclusion
    -   a series of steps to be taken
    -   dates that steps must be completed

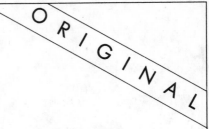

TO: Calliope Stanyan   DATE: June 19, 1998

DEPT: Corporate Legal   FROM: Walter Frank

SUBJECT: Zita Tribula's Settlement

As you know, a great deal of effort was done by our department and with
Personnel in securing a fair settlement of the discrimination charge filed
by Zita Tribula in which she alleged that she was not given a permanent
secretarial position because of her national origin. The proposed
negotiated settlement which was approved by both the Equal Opportunity
Specialist and his supervising attorney at the EEOC was contested by WOE
(Women Organized for Employment) who have been acting as spokespersons for
Ms. Tribula. Ms. Tribula was given thirty days to accept or reject the
negotiated settlement offer which the EEOC determined was full remedy. Ms.
Tribula and WOE were able to convince higher authorities within the EEOC
that the settlement was not full remedy. I have now been contacted by the
Assistant Director for the Regional Office that Ms. Tribula will not accept
the offer which we proposed and the EEOC feels that there is justification
to proceed with some type of investigation. I am to receive some
interrogatories in a few days in which we are to clarify our position as to
the allegations made by Ms. Tribula. In speaking with the Assistant
Director he made it clear that he has only been exposed to the information
supplied by Ms. Tribula and we will have the opportunity to rebut her
allegations before a determination is made. The Assistant Director has
suggested that we increase our offer, possibly to a Grade 9 secretarial
position in order to placate Ms. Tribula.

In addition to the points made above, I need your assistance in determining
what to do with the position which Personnel had set aside for Ms. Tribula
in our efforts to place her. Personnel has requested that we supply them
with a memorandum in which we approve of their filling the position left
vacant for Ms. Tribula with someone else. Their request seems more than
reasonable but I would like your approval before proceeding. Could we
discuss this matter on Monday, June 22?

WHAT TO DO

Creating headings for your exploratory writing is a valuable way to organize your ideas. The writer of this original told all he knew about Zita Tribula's case. Let's help the reader understand it.

1. First, using what you have learned under "Purpose Up Front," locate the key request of the memo and underline it.

2. Now read through the memo. Every time the subject changes, put a slash.

3. Write a heading for each section.

4. Under each heading, underline what the reader needs to know. (Discard the rest.)

5. Put the headings in a logical sequence by writing a number in the margin: 1, 2, 3, etc.

TO: Calliope Stanyan   **DATE:** June 19, 1998

DEPT: Corporate Legal   **FROM:** Walter Frank

SUBJECT: Zita Tribula's Settlement

As you know, a great deal of effort was done by our department and with Personnel in securing a fair settlement of the discrimination charge filed by Zita Tribula in which she alleged that she was not given a permanent secretarial position because of her national origin. The proposed negotiated settlement which was approved by both the Equal Opportunity Specialist and his supervising attorney at the EEOC was contested by WOE (Women Organized for Employment) who have been acting as spokespersons for Ms. Tribula. Ms. Tribula was given thirty days to accept or reject the negotiated settlement offer which the EEOC determined was full remedy. Ms. Tribula and WOE were able to convince higher authorities within the EEOC that the settlement was not full remedy. I have now been contacted by the Assistant Director for the Regional Office that Ms. Tribula will not accept the offer which we proposed and the EEOC feels that there is justification to proceed with some type of investigation. I am to receive some interrogatories in a few days in which we are to clarify our position as to the allegations made by Ms. Tribula. In speaking with the Assistant Director he made it clear that he has only been exposed to the information supplied by Ms. Tribula and we will have the opportunity to rebut her allegations before a determination is made. The Assistant Director has suggested that we increase our offer, possibly to a Grade 9 secretarial position in order to placate Ms. Tribula.

In addition to the points made above, I need your assistance in determining what to do with the position which Personnel had set aside for Ms. Tribula in our efforts to place her. Personnel has requested that we supply them with a memorandum in which we approve of their filling the position left vacant for Ms. Tribula with someone else. Their request seems more than reasonable but I would like your approval before proceeding. Could we discuss this matter on Monday, June 22?

ANSWERS

1. Purpose up front: The writer wants to meet with the reader. Put this in the first sentence so it can't be overlooked. An innocent-looking "report" on a completed settlement might get filed after a quick glance, and valuable time would be lost while the writer waits for the reader's decision.

2–5. See our rewrite on the next page.

•   •   •   •

OUR REWRITE

SUBJECT CHANGED FROM   Zita Tribula's
Settlement
TO   Zita Tribula's
Rejection
of Settlement

HEADINGS are flares. By reading just twenty-three words, the reader grasps the situation and is ready to act.

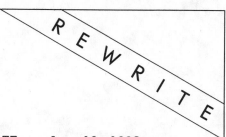

TO: Calliope Stanyan   DATE: June 19, 1998

FROM: Walter Frank, Corporate Legal

SUBJECT: Zita Tribula's Rejection of Settlement

FOR: [ ] action   [X] decision   [ ] information

Could we get together on Monday, June 22? We are now coming to some crucial decisions on the case of Zita Tribula, who alleges that she was rejected for a permanent secretarial position because of her national origin.

Negotiations have broken down

Ms. Tribula has rejected the proposed EEOC—negotiated settlement which was approved by both the Equal Opportunity Specialist and his supervising attorney at the EEOC. She had 30 days to accept or reject it. However, during that time, WOE (Women Organized for Employment), which has been speaking for Ms. Tribula, convinced higher authorities within EEOC that the settlement was not full remedy.

We must respond to new investigation

We will receive some interrogatories in a few days in which we can clarify our position. The assistant director for the regional EEOC office assures me that while he feels there is justification to proceed with an investigation, we will have the opportunity to rebut Ms. Tribula's allegations.

Decisions to be made

1. Shall we increase our offer to Ms. Tribula?

    The regional EEOC director suggests that we place her with an increased offer, possibly to a grade 9 secretarial position.

2. Shall we fill her vacancy?

    Personnel requests a memorandum authorizing them to place someone else in the position that has been held vacant for Ms. Tribula and which she has now refused. This seems reasonable, but I would like your approval before proceeding.

SOME COMMON ERRORS

What You Say	What You Think You're Saying	What You're Really Saying
enormity	immensity	hideous cruelty
dearth	lots of	complete lack of
antidote	amusing story (*anecdote*)	remedy for poison
cite	location (*site*)	quote, refer to
flare	talent for (*flair*)	bright light
specious	improbable	deceptive
wave (a claim)	relinquish (*waive*)	move back and forth

CHAPTER 5

Verbs

 What do you want done?

Sometimes we try so hard to be diplomatic that we don't say directly what we want done or whom we want to do it. We think our artfully phrased desires will be instantly interpreted and acted on.

Too often such diplomacy only leads to frustration and waste. Remember that directness does not equal brusqueness. Rudeness, imperiousness, or callousness can lurk in the most flowery language.

Say why you are writing simply and quickly. When too many important points are swirling in your mind, it helps to start like this:

The purpose of this memo is to . . .

In fact, if too many of your interoffice communications have you muttering "Why are you telling me all this?" it may help to have this inscribed at the top of your memo forms.

Active Verbs

English uses two kinds of verbs, transitive (direct, acting on something) and intransitive (indirect, passive). Learn to use direct, transitive, action verbs.

SAY: Sam should turn off the lights when he leaves.

NOT: The lights should be turned off when leaving.

SAY: File these tax forms by Friday to avoid a penalty.

NOT: The new IRS ruling requires immediate response.

Use specific names or titles—Sam, Personnel Department, "all vice presidents"—so everyone knows who is being asked or told to do what.

USE ACTIVE LANGUAGE

Passive	Active
should be done	please do
must be submitted	submit by (date)
action should be taken	take action
forms go to Receiving	Bill, send the forms to Receiving
should be discussed	Let's discuss Thursday
in a timely manner	Call me by Tuesday if you can't finish the job by May 10

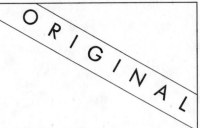

TO: Regional Personnel Managers   DATE: December 23, 1999

SUBJECT: Code of Ethics Statement

FROM: R. Nixon

DEPT: Industrial Relations

Manual Change No. 78 implements a policy requiring that all local payroll employees involved in purchasing goods or services sign a Code of Ethics Statement. This policy applies to current employees as well as new hires. Employees such as head mechanics, shop managers or supervisors, maintenance supervisors and anyone else who deals with outside sources for the purchase of goods or services are required to read the World—Wide Code of Business Ethics and the Code of Ethics Statement and sign the statement. A copy of the signed statement should be placed in the employee's file.

Please give me a call if you have any questions.

Wʜᴀᴛ ᴛᴏ ᴅᴏ

Here is a dramatic example of someone who is offering important information but is too polite to ask directly that anyone do anything. The readers must infer their instructions.

1. Put a check next to who is supposed to do something.

2. Does the memo say how all these people will know what to do?

3. Underline what is supposed to be done.

4. Circle any supports, background, explanations of why this must be done.

TO: Regional Personnel Managers   DATE: December 23, 1999

SUBJECT: Code of Ethics Statement   FROM: R. Nixon

DEPT: Industrial Relations

Manual Change No. 78 implements a policy requiring that all local payroll employees involved in purchasing goods or services sign a Code of Ethics Statement. This policy applies to current employees as well as new hires. Employees such as head mechanics, shop managers or supervisors, maintenance supervisors and anyone else who deals with outside sources for the purchase of goods or services are required to read the World-Wide Code of Business Ethics and the Code of Ethics Statement and sign the statement. A copy of the signed statement should be placed in the employee's file.

Please give me a call if you have any questions.

ANSWERS

1. Something is supposed to be done by "current employees as well as new hires. Employees such as head mechanics, shop managers or supervisors, maintenance supervisors and anyone else who deals with outside sources for the purchase of goods or services."

2. No, the memo does not explain how people will know what to do.

3. The original uses indirect verbs to describe what is supposed to be done: ". . . are required to read the World-Wide Code of Business Ethics and the Code of Ethics Statement and sign the statement. A copy of the signed statement should be placed in the employee's file."

4. The support—the reason employees should sign the Code of Ethics Statement—is: "Manual Change No. 78 implements a policy requiring that all local payroll employees involved in purchasing goods or services sign a Code of Ethics Statement."

• • • •

OUR REWRITE

SUBJECT
CHANGED FROM   Code of Ethics Statement

TO   Using the New Code of Ethics Statement

RESPONSE DATE   added ("Effective immediately...").

TONE: Obviously the writer is concerned about the sensitivity of the issue, but his passive verbs may result in confusion, noncompliance, and even eventual ill will. We have substituted active verbs.

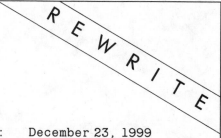

TO: Regional Personnel Managers   DATE: December 23, 1999

FROM: R. Nixon, Industrial Relations

SUBJECT: Using the New Code of Ethics Statement

FOR: [X] action   [ ] decision   [ ] information

Effective immediately, please have all local payroll employees and new hires <u>who are involved in purchasing goods or services</u> sign a Code of Ethics Statement. (Manual Change No. 78)

1. Explain to them that they are required to read and sign the World–Wide Code of Business Ethics and the Code of Ethics Statement.

2. Have them read and sign the statement.

3. Place a copy in their personnel file.

Give me a call if you have any questions.

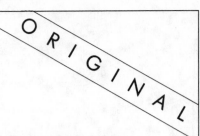

TO: Gilda Fletcher   DATE: January 14, 1998

FROM: Chuck DeWitt   .

SUBJECT: Plans for Planning Session

Gilda, attached you will find the planning issues that have been identified
as a means toward building a strong Managerial unit within your department.

I believe our agreement to have a one day off—site planning meeting will
provide the time required to effectively deal with the identified issues.

In addition to discussion of the issues, I would suggest that in the course
of the day we include a self—administered questionnaire that helps
individuals be aware of their communication style and how we can manage our
preferred style of communication for successful results in a variety of
work settings. This information would provide a base for each person to
understand him or herself in the SPECTOR environment.

I cannot meet on any of the following dates: January 18, 25, 26, 27 or
February 1, 8, 12, 15, 19 or 22. I would be willing to meet on a Saturday or a
Sunday, but I am not free February 6/7, February 13/14 nor February 20/21
due to other commitments. I will try to hold free the remaining dates until
I hear from you so I'll need a quick response!

Once we establish a date, you and I should have a brief session to discuss
our roles and a meeting design for the day.

WHAT TO DO

1. The subject is "Plans for Planning Session." Write a clearer title here.

2. Who is being asked to do what?

3. When should they meet? (Note that the writer lists dates when he *can't* meet with Ms. Fletcher, but what about when he *can*?)

TO: Gilda Fletcher   DATE: January 14, 1998

FROM: Chuck DeWitt

SUBJECT: Plans for Planning Session

Gilda, attached you will find the planning issues that have been identified as a means toward building a strong Managerial unit within your department.

I believe our agreement to have a one day off-site planning meeting will provide the time required to effectively deal with the identified issues.

In addition to discussion of the issues, I would suggest that in the course of the day we include a self-administered questionnaire that helps individuals be aware of their communication style and how we can manage our preferred style of communication for successful results in a variety of work settings. This information would provide a base for each person to understand him or herself in the SPECTOR environment.

I cannot meet on any of the following dates: January 18, 25, 26, 27 or February 1, 8, 12, 15, 19 or 22. I would be willing to meet on a Saturday or a Sunday, but I am not free February 6/7, February 13/14 nor February 20/21 due to other commitments. I will try to hold free the remaining dates until I hear from you so I'll need a quick response!

Once we establish a date, you and I should have a brief session to discuss our roles and a meeting design for the day.

ANSWERS

1. **SUBJECT**
   CHANGED FROM   Plans for Planning Session

   TO   Preparation for Off-Site Planning Meeting

2. Reader is being asked to do four things. (See rewrite.)

3. Arbitrary possible dates for meeting are offered. Listing dates that are *not* good for a meeting is less efficient than giving several alternate dates that *are* good.

•   •   •   •

OUR REWRITE

VERBS   in the headings identify the steps to be taken:

> *set* a date
> *review*
> *consider*
> *meet*

SUBJECT   clarified. (See above.)

ATTACHMENTS   added and described. The writer should include a copy of the questionnaire instead of describing it.

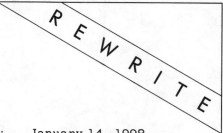

TO: Gilda Fletcher   DATE: January 14, 1998

FROM: Chuck DeWitt

SUBJECT: Preparation for Off—Site Planning Meeting

FOR: [ ] action   [X] decision   [ ] information

We need to identify the next steps in preparation for the one—day off—site planning meeting. Please:

1. <u>Immediately set a date for the meeting</u>.
    How about one of the following?
    January 20
    January 29
    February 5
    February 17

2. <u>Review</u> the attached planning issues.

3. <u>Consider</u> using a self—administered communications questionnaire during the off—site meeting. A sample is attached.

4. <u>Meet with me for a preliminary discussion</u> as soon as we have established the session date. We'll decide on our roles and a meeting design.

Att: List of planning issues
      Sample communications questionnaire

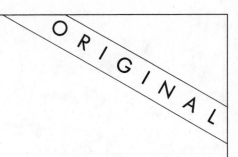

May 1, 1999

    TO: Arthur Marx

  FROM: Allan Jones (for Sam Wood)

    RE: Request for Office Move

1) We wish to have Kate Carlisle and Walter Woolf exchange offices.

2) We wish to have Julius Marx move from his current modular space to the desk directly across from Margaret Dumont.

3) With respect to the above three moves, we are requesting that all telephone extension numbers move with the person so that there will be no change in directory information, and further, that both Julius Marx and Kate Carlisle's extensions be added to the executive call group. If this is not possible, please let me know. An alternative would be to have Sylvia and Marge added to the call group of Sig Rumann and Billy Gilbert.

4) We are currently using the modular unit formerly occupied by Billy Gilbert as a work/filing room. We would like to discuss changing this space so that a door opens into the executive area. Please call me so that we can set up an appointment to discuss this. In addition, we would like to have a phone placed in this room, with a nonpublished extension number. Sam requests that all parties involved in these moves be notified well in advance of the move and that they be provided with any facilities help to coordinate the move effectively (such as boxes, if required).

With regard to 1), 2), and 3) above, please notify me of when this move can take place along with a firm move date.

Thank you for your support.

cc: Sam Wood
    Kate Carlisle
    Walter Woolf
    Julius Marx
    Margaret Dumont
    George S. Kaufman
    Morrie Ryskind

WHAT TO DO

When many things are happening at once, it is often difficult to move through the information in a logical sequence. Here's where good business writing can help you organize your thoughts and approach your non-writing activities in a more orderly and productive way.

The original memo here is a list of requests, neatly numbered. Could the list be clearer? Will clarifying the list help the writer (and the reader) make decisions and organize their actions more efficiently?

1. Put a check next to each request.

2. Does this list suggest some general headings that you could group the separate requests under? Jot some possibilities below.

3. The writer is asking the reader's approval for this list. He also asks for something else that logically should precede this approval. Find this "hidden" request and underline it.

ORIGINAL

May 1, 1999

TO: Arthur Marx

FROM: Allan Jones (for Sam Wood)

RE: Request for Office Move

1) We wish to have Kate Carlisle and Walter Woolf exchange offices.

2) We wish to have Julius Marx move from his current modular space to the desk directly across from Margaret Dumont.

3) With respect to the above three moves, we are requesting that all telephone extension numbers move with the person so that there will be no change in directory information, and _further_, that both Julius Marx and Kate Carlisle's extensions be added to the executive call group. If this is not possible, please let me know. An alternative would be to have Sylvia and Marge added to the call group of Sig Rumann and Billy Gilbert.

4) We are currently using the modular unit formerly occupied by Billy Gilbert as a work/filing room. We would like to discuss changing this space so that a door opens into the executive area. Please call me so that we can set up an appointment to discuss this. In addition, we would like to have a phone placed in this room, with a nonpublished extension number. Sam requests that all parties involved in these moves be notified well in advance of the move and that they be provided with any facilities help to coordinate the move effectively (such as boxes, if required).

With regard to 1), 2), and 3) above, please notify me of when this move can take place along with a firm move date.

Thank you for your support.

cc: Sam Wood
     Kate Carlisle
     Walter Woolf
     Julius Marx
     Margaret Dumont
     George S. Kaufman
     Morrie Ryskind

ANSWERS

1. The requests appear in the rewrite as the five numbered items plus the request for a new door.

2. Headings suggested by the separate requests are:
   > Moves
   > Phone Changes
   > New Door

3. In item 4 the writer asks the reader to call him to set up an appointment to discuss adding a door and an unlisted telephone.

• • • •

OUR REWRITE

The writer of the original memo lists some requested changes and asks the reader to notify him when the requested move can take place. But in item 4 he asks for a meeting to discuss adding a door and an unlisted telephone. Then he asks for boxes to help with the move.

More logically, he should start by asking for the meeting. Even if much of this has been discussed before, going over the precise points of the rewrite will nail down all the issues and suggest a logical procedure. Asking for a ''firm move date'' and boxes (final two paragraphs of original) is probably premature.

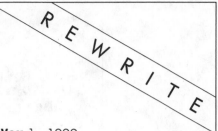

```
     TO:    Arthur Marx            DATE:   May 1, 1999

    FROM:   Allan Jones (for Sam Wood)   CC:   Sam Wood
                                               Kate Carlisle
                                               Walter Woolf
                                               Julius Marx
                                               Margaret Dumont
                                               George S. Kaufman
                                               Morrie Ryskind


  SUBJECT:   Request for Office Move

     FOR:    [ ] action   [X] decision   [ ] information
```

We would like your approval for the following changes in our work space. Can we meet next Thursday or Friday morning to discuss the details? Please call me to confirm a time.

Moves

1. Kate Carlisle and Walter Woolf would exchange offices.

2. Julius Marx would move from his current modular space to the desk directly across from Margaret Dumont.

Phone Changes

1. Move each person's current extension number to his new location, so directory information remains the same.

2. EITHER: Add extensions for Julius and Kate to the executive call group.
    OR: If this is not possible, add Sylvia and Marge to the call group of Sig Rumann and Billy Gilbert.

3. Add a telephone with an unlisted number in the current work/storage area. (See below.)

New Door

We want to discuss adding a door between the executive area and the modular unit space formerly occupied by Gilbert and now used as a work/filing storage room.

SHORT AND CONCISE

Before	After
Enclosed please find	Here is
	Enclosed is
Due to the fact that	Because
It is important to add that	But
	Also
	. . . as well.
It is interesting to point out that	Interestingly
those in the employ of ABC	ABC employees
is impactful	is effective
	will affect
conceptualize	conceive, think, plan, imagine, decide (be more precise!)
potentialities	potential
Pursuant to our agreement	We agreed that
	Our agreement says
Please be advised that your rates will increase	Your rates will increase
Henceforth	Starting today
in regards to	about
	for
in order to simplify	to simplify
	so we can simplify
A question must be asked as to the reason for	Why is
upon completion of your audits	when you finish your audits
at that point in time	then
as per our discussion	as we discussed

CHAPTER 6

Short Paragraphs and Sentences

 Is your writing easy to read?

When you talk, the tone of your voice, your pauses and inflections, can mean as much as your words. You provide natural separations to display your ideas.

When you write, the visual appeal of the page can encourage your reader, pulling his eye from point to point. Or it can sabotage you entirely.

If you don't type your own correspondence, you may feel that this is something "the secretary should take care of." Of course, having a brilliant editor and layout artist who also types is helpful, but good format starts with good organization, and that starts with you.

TO: Regional Training Managers   DATE: August 13, 1995

FROM: John Palmer

SUBJECT: REGIONAL TRAINING MANAGERS' MEETING

It's time, in fact we're overdue, to have another combined meeting of Regional Training Managers and Home Office Training and Education Department personnel. What with training new hires, EOE classes, new products and so forth, it remains as usual a very difficult task to schedule a time when we can meet, but somehow we must. According to my calculations, the last week in October is probably the best time available for a meeting. Without getting involved at this point in agenda times, I'd like to first check to make sure this is a workable time for each of you. Please check your appointment books and determine if October 28—30 are good dates, with October 27 and 31 being travel days.

As always, I'm sure there will be more to discuss than time will allow, so prioritization of subjects will be most important. After checking your appointment schedule to make sure these dates are clear, please let me know, and if you're so inclined, jot down some subjects you'd like placed on the agenda. If possible, please have your comments on the agenda and your "green light" on the dates back to me by September 12 or sooner. Thanks much.

cc: R. Cory
     J. Hirschfeld
     Regional Managers

WHAT TO DO

It is easy to shorten the long paragraphs of this chunky original.

1. Underline what the reader needs to know.

2. Synthesize the information and summarize it here.

TO: Regional Training Managers   DATE: August 13, 1995

FROM: John Palmer

SUBJECT: REGIONAL TRAINING MANAGERS' MEETING

It's time, in fact we're overdue, to have another combined meeting of Regional Training Managers and Home Office Training and Education Department personnel. What with training new hires, EOE classes, new products and so forth, it remains as usual a very difficult task to schedule a time when we can meet, but somehow we must. According to my calculations, the last week in October is probably the best time available for a meeting. Without getting involved at this point in agenda items, I'd like to first check to make sure this is a workable time for each of you. Please check your appointment books and determine if October 28–30 are good dates, with October 27 and 31 being travel days.

As always, I'm sure there will be more to discuss than time will allow, so prioritization of subjects will be most important. After checking your appointment schedule to make sure these dates are clear, please let me know, and if you're so inclined, jot down some subjects you'd like placed on the agenda. If possible, please have your comments on the agenda and your "green light" on the dates back to me by September 12 or sooner. Thanks much.

cc: R. Cory
    J. Hirschfeld
    Regional Managers

ANSWERS

1. You were probably tempted to underline much of the original memo because the writer was being quite chatty and using intransitive verbs. The information the reader *really* needs is underlined below:

> It's time, in fact we're overdue, <u>to have another combined meeting of Regional Training Managers and Home Office Training and Education Department personnel</u>. What with training new hires, EOE classes, new products and so forth, it remains as usual a very difficult task to schedule a time when we can meet, but somehow we must. According to my calculations, <u>the last week in October is probably the best time available for a meeting</u>. Without getting involved at this point in agenda items, I'd like to first check to make sure this is a workable time for each of you. <u>Please check your appointment books and determine if October 28–30 are good dates</u>, with October 27 and 31 being travel days.
>
> As always, I'm sure there will be more to discuss than time will allow, so prioritization of subjects will be most important. After checking your appointment schedule to make sure these dates are clear, <u>please let me know</u>, and if you're so inclined, jot down <u>some subjects you'd like placed on the agenda</u>. If possible, please <u>have your comments on the agenda and your "green light" on the dates back to me by September 12 or sooner</u>. Thanks much.

2. For a summary of the writer's wishes, see the rewrite opposite.

•   •   •   •   •

OUR REWRITE

SUBJECT CHANGED FROM   Regional Training Managers' Meeting

TO   Scheduling Regional Training Managers' Meeting

TONE: The writer wants to sound friendly, but making people wade through hundreds of words to find out why you are writing isn't kindness. Brevity can be warm and cheerful too.

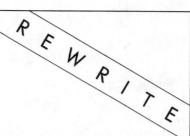

```
      TO:   Regional Training Managers   DATE:   August 13, 1995

    FROM:   John Palmer                    CC:    Regional Managers
                                                  R. Cory
                                                  J. Hirschfeld

 SUBJECT:   Scheduling Regional Training Managers' Meeting

     FOR:   [ ] action   [X] decision   [ ] information
```

Can we get together the last week in October for an overdue combined meeting of Regional Training Managers and Home Office Training and Educational Department personnel?

Please let me know by <u>September 12</u>:

1. If you're available October 28—30 (with October 27 and 31 as travel days)

2. What you'd like to see on the agenda

Any time you think you need pages and pages to "sell" someone, think about the power of an artfully prepared ten-second commercial.

To sell anything—an idea, a product, yourself—be brief!

CHAPTER 7

Attachments

 Will your writing be easier to understand if you put background information, schedules, instructions, charts, etc., in attachments?

"Attachments" is not a synonym for "garbage"! Admittedly it's very tempting to put all the leftovers in a bunch and label them "Attachments" (or, for letters, "Enclosures").

Don't. Attachments can be a powerful tool if you think of them as supports. They should back up your main communication. Typical supports could contain:

- background information (history, procedures, rules, etc.)
- legal, social, financial considerations
- statistics
- related documents
- outside opinions and recommendations

Using these supports as attachments rather than quoting them in the body of your writing allows you to emphasize your main points in a shorter, crisper communication.

TO: Bob Hickson, Risk & Insurance Mgt.   DATE: April 9, 1999

FROM: R. Davis, EEO Relations

SUBJECT: PREEMPLOYMENT PHYSICALS

In response to the request you made on March 9, 1999, at the Preemployment
Physical Meeting, I am forwarding to you a discussion of the laws
concerning preemployment physicals. Since it is in my area of
responsibility to ensure compliance with state and federal equal
employment opportunity laws and regulations, I researched the areas of the
laws applicable to preemployment physicals to assure that our focus and our
action in protecting the Company would not constitute a violation of our
obligation to employ the qualified handicapped. Following is an analysis
and summary of my findings.

If my memory serves me correctly, the concerns expressed at the meeting
were based on one or more of the following: 1. An applicant may not be
physically able to perform the required job duties; 2. An applicant may
become incapacitated at some time in the future; 3. The job duties may cause
the applicant's condition to worsen, resulting in a work-related injury
suit for disability payments; and 4. The applicant's condition may
increase the possibility that he or she would receive a serious work
injury, resulting in a lawsuit and greater insurance liability.

The above considerations have been tempered by amendments to civil rights
laws in over 30 states prohibiting discrimination based on a physical
handicap unless it reasonably prevents the person from doing the job.
Because Spector is a federal contractor, I will concern myself primarily
with the Rehabilitation Act of 1995 (hereinafter referred to as "the
Act"). The matter of preemployment physicals involves the interpretation
and construction of Section 503 of the Act which, if violated, could result
in administrative penalties, including termination of federal contracts or
debarment from future contracts.

For purposes of the Act, a handicapped individual is a person "who has a
physical or mental impairment which substantially limits one or more of
such person's major life activities." Such a limitation, according to

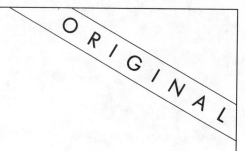

the Act, is evidenced if the individual is likely to experience difficulty in securing, retaining, or advancing in employment because of a handicap. The Act also considers handicapped those individuals who have a record of such an impairment or who are "regarded as having" an impairment. An individual who may be completely recovered from a previous physical impairment (such as heart attack, cancer) for example, often has difficulty in job situations because of his handicap history and as such, receives protection under the Act. According to this definition, the following may result in a discrimination complaint if persons are rejected from employment because of them: having only one arm, being an epileptic, having had rheumatic fever as a child, having had a heart attack, having high blood pressure, and being obese. Denying a person a job because of these conditions, or record of having such a condition, could be unlawful.

1. AN APPLICANT MAY NOT BE PHYSICALLY ABLE TO PERFORM THE REQUIRED JOB
    DUTIES:

Nothing in the Act prohibits an employer from requiring all applicants and employees, including those identified as handicapped individuals, to undergo medical examinations at the expense of the employer. Moreover, the employer can limit exams to certain jobs. However, the employer CANNOT use the results of the medical examination to exclude or limit the opportunities of qualified handicapped individuals. The medical examinations should be given to determine proper placement and accommodations and not to screen out qualified handicapped applicants. The government requires employers covered by Section 503 to "make reasonable accommodation to the physical and mental limitations" of employees and applicants who may be handicapped. Reasonable accommodation means the changes and modifications which can be made in the structure of a job or in the manner in which a job is performed unless it would impose an undue hardship on the conduct of the business. Reasonable job accommodations cannot be denied to a handicapped applicant who would be qualified to do the job with some accommodations. (This prohibition does not apply to those employers located in about a dozen states not having such laws and who have no federal contracts over $2,500.) This obligation includes both alterations in the structure or scheduling of a job. Currently there are no

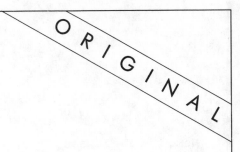

definitive standards for what constitutes reasonable accommodation. Such factors as "business necessity" and "financial cost and expenses" are taken into account.

2. AN APPLICANT MAY BECOME INCAPACITATED AT SOME TIME IN THE FUTURE:

Upholding a 1979 Labor Department ruling, Judge Samuel King, a Federal District Judge in Honolulu, Hawaii, ruled that E.E. Black, Ltd., (E.E. Black, Ltd. v. Marshall, 23 FEP 1253) a construction firm was wrong in turning down apprentice carpenter George Crosby by claiming he was "unqualified" because he risked injury. While noting such a risk may be a legitimate factor in hiring, King said it should not be used to "make an otherwise capable person incapable." "Non-imminent risk of future injury may possibly be a reason for rejecting an applicant, but it does not make an otherwise capable person incapable," King said. According to King, the only relevant inquiry in determining whether a rejected applicant is a qualified applicant is whether the applicant was capable of performing the job at the time he was rejected. "In some cases, the risk of injury may be so immediate as to prevent an individual from being considered presently capable of performing a particular job. This is not the case." Thus, the Court found that Mr. Crosby was a qualified handicapped individual as that term is used in Section 503 of the Act, and as that term is defined in other sections of the Act and the regulations.

3. THE JOB DUTIES MAY CAUSE THE APPLICANT'S CONDITION TO WORSEN, RESULTING IN A WORK-RELATED INJURY SUIT FOR DISABILITY PAYMENTS:

After requiring ALL applicants for apprentice carpenter to take the preemployment physical, E.E. Black rejected Crosby for employment in 1976 because of his negative back X-ray which made him a "poor risk for heavy labor," according to the company doctor. Crosby had a 75% to 80% chance of developing future back problems if he continued to perform heavy labor, the doctor predicted. The Court said "a construction worker with a congenital back condition" is a " 'qualified handicapped individual' and should not be rejected from employment because of the risk of potential injury to himself."

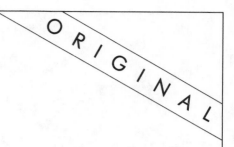

4.   THE APPLICANT'S CONDITION MAY INCREASE THE POSSIBILITY THAT HE OR SHE
      WOULD RECEIVE A SERIOUS WORK INJURY, RESULTING IN A LAWSUIT AND GREATER
      INSURANCE LIABILITY:

On the propriety of rejecting Mr. Crosby because of the risk of future
injury and increased insurance or workers' compensation costs, the Court
in referring to the findings of the Assistant Secretary of the Department
of Labor, that the risk of future injury because of a physical or mental
condition can never be the basis for rejecting a qualified handicapped
individual, irrespective of the likelihood of injury, the seriousness of
the possible injury or the imminence of the injury, had this to say: "SUCH A
HOLDING IS CONTRARY TO LAW." (Emphasis added). The Secretary's position
was that at best Black had shown that Mr. Crosby's condition had a potential
for future significance, and was not related to his current capacity to
perform; and, that possible cost increases in insurance of workers'
compensation costs were irrelevant. The Court went on to say: "(If) for
example, it was determined that if a particular person were given a
particular job, he would have a 90% chance of suffering a heart attack
within one month, that clearly would be a valid reason for denying that
individual the job, notwithstanding his status as a qualified handicapped
individual. A job requirement that screened out such an individual would be
consistent with business necessity and the safe performance of the job.
Yet, it could be argued that the individual had a current capacity to
perform the job, and thus was a qualified handicapped individual."
However, the Court also indicated that it would not formulate a legal
standard, but would proceed on a case by case basis. And, in the largest
Rehabilitation Act settlement to date, Varo Semiconductor Company recently
agreed to pay $225,000 to 85 applicants allegedly denied employment
because they were handicapped. The settlement resolved claims that the
company SYSTEMATICALLY (emphasis added) used its preemployment physical
examinations to disqualify applicants for such conditions as obesity,
color blindness, arthritis, hypertension, allergies, and varicose veins.
Interestingly the case focused attention on the Department of Labor's
controversial definition of "handicap" as any physically disqualifying
factor.

Where do we go from here? In summary, it seems clear to me that we must focus
attention, not only on whether the applicant is qualified to do the job, or
whether the applicant can safely perform the task, but also on whether we

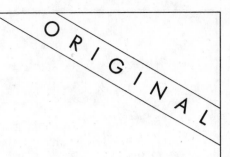

Memo to Bob Hickson
April 9, 1999
Page 5

can make reasonable accommodation for THAT applicant. Finally, we should
bear in mind that "(T)he threat of federal intervention" in our business
when an aggrieved handicapped individual files a complaint with the Labor
Department to remedy a violation of Section 503 "is a special kind of
leverage" that can be "a tool of uncommon power." (Trial, February 1981,
Association of Trial Lawyers of America, 1050 31st St., N.W., Washington,
D.C.)

RD:ed

cc: Christopher West
     Kyra Minninger
     Yuki Nakamura
     Charlotte Milton
     Richard Stookey

WHAT TO DO

This overwhelming memo contains much valuable information . . . if you could absorb it.

Four problem areas were discussed at a meeting. They are listed in paragraph two of page one, then treated more extensively on the next three pages.

1. This memo discusses four health issues that may or may not affect hiring. They are numbered 1 to 4. In order to create an easy-to-read summary of all four on the first page of your rewrite, underline the key point in the long paragraph following each of the four points.

2. Put a check next to information that could go in an attachment called: "Definitions from the Rehabilitation Act of 1995."

3. Put an "X" next to information that could be put in an attachment called: "Court Decisions." Then create subheadings for each different aspect.

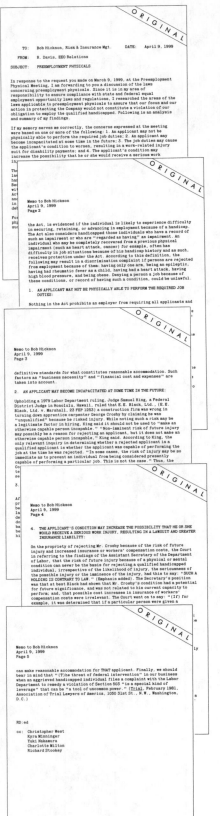

ANSWERS

1. The key information under each of the four health issues of the original memo appears in the first-page summary of the rewrite on the opposite page.

2. Definitions from the Rehabilitation Act of 1995 have been collected in Attachment 1.

3. Court decisions have been collected and given subheadings in Attachment 2.

• • • •

OUR REWRITE

SUBJECT CHANGED FROM   Preemployment Physicals

TO   Legal Issues of Preemployment Physicals

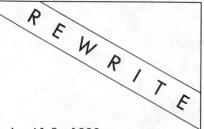

TO: Bob Hickson, Risk & Insurance   DATE: April 9, 1999

FROM: R. Davis, EEO Relations   CC: Christopher West
                                            Kyra Minninger
                                            Yuki Nakamura
SUBJECT: Legal Issues of Preemployment   Charlotte Milton
         Physicals   Richard Stookey

FOR: [ ] action   [ ] decision   [X] information

Four problem areas of preemployment physical examinations for the handicapped were discussed at our March 12 meeting. The law seems to be as follows:

1. <u>When an applicant may seem physically unable to perform the required job duties</u>, the employer is still obliged to make "reasonable" changes whenever possible to adapt the job to his handicap.

2. <u>When an applicant may be expected to become more severely handicapped in the future</u>, such "nonimminent" risk cannot disqualify him from employment in the present.

3. <u>Even if the job duties themselves may cause the applicant's condition to worsen</u>, the applicant cannot be rejected because of the threat of injury that is merely "potential."

4. <u>Even if the job duties carry the risk of serious work injury</u>, the applicant must still be considered qualified as long as he has a "current capacity" to perform the job.

<u>Penalties</u>: Section 503 of the Rehabilitation Act imposes serious penalties, including loss of federal contracts, on violators. Therefore, we must take care that our policy of preemployment physicals does not result in "systematic discrimination."

ATTACHMENTS: 1. Definitions from Rehabilitation Act of 1995
              2. Court Decisions

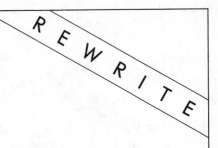

ATTACHMENT 1

Definitions from Rehabilitation Act of 1995

Qualified Handicapped Individuals

For the purposes of the Rehabilitation Act of 1995, a handicapped individual is one "who has a physical or mental impairment which substantially limits one or more of such person's major life activities," and also those who have a record of such an impairment, or who are "regarded as having" an impairment. Someone who has completely recovered from a heart attack or cancer, for example, is often treated as handicapped when applying for employment, and is therefore protected by the Act. Likewise, persons with a missing limb or epilepsy or high blood pressure are protected. It may even be possible in some situations to extend such protection to people with obesity, color blindness, arthritis, hypertension, allergies, or varicose veins.

Reasonable Accommodation

At present, there are no definitive standards for what constitutes reasonable accommodation. In general, the term may refer to alterations in physical facilities, or modifications in the structure or scheduling of a job, or both.

The Rehabilitation Act and Preemployment Physicals

Nothing in the Act prohibits preemployment physicals, whether for all employment or for specific jobs. However, such exams may not be used to exclude or limit the opportunities of qualified handicapped individuals. Rather, they should be given to determine proper placement and "reasonable accommodation to the physical and mental limitations" of handicapped employees and applicants.

Penalties for Violations

For companies such as Spector which have federal contracts over $2,500, penalties may include termination of such contracts or debarment from future contracts.

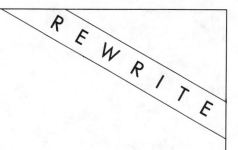

ATTACHMENT 2

Court Decisions

E. E. BLACK LTD. v. MARSHALL (23 FEP 1253)

This case, held in Federal District Court, Honolulu, Hawaii, upheld a 1979 Labor Department ruling. But the Court refused to formulate a legal standard, preferring to proceed on a case-by-case basis.

   <u>Background</u>: In 1976, Black had rejected apprentice carpenter George Crosby for employment because of a back X ray which indicated that he was a "poor risk for heavy labor." According to the company doctor, Crosby stood a 75% to 80% chance of developing future back problems if he were employed to do such work.

   <u>Quotes from Decision</u>: Judge Samuel King noted that such a risk may be a legitimate factor in hiring, but found that a

   non-imminent risk of future injury . . . does not make an otherwise capable person incapable.

King further ruled that the only relevant inquiry in determining whether an applicant was qualified was whether he was capable of performing the job at the time he was rejected:

   In some cases, the risk of injury may be so immediate as to prevent an individual from being considered presently capable of performing a particular job. This is not the case.

The Court also referred to the findings of the assistant secretary of the Department of Labor:

   . . . that the risk of future injury because of a physical or mental condition can never be the basis for rejecting a qualified handicapped individual, however likely or serious or imminent the injury; and that to disqualify an applicant for such cause is contrary to law.

The Court then considered the propriety of employing a particular person for a job when the applicant "would have a 90% chance of suffering a heart attack within one month." In such a case, Judge King suggested that there would be:

   a valid reason for denying that individual the job . . . A job requirement that screened out such an individual <u>would be consistent with business necessity and the safe performance of the job</u>. [emphasis added]

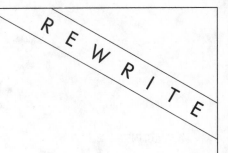

ATTACHMENT 2—continued

Yet the Court said it could also be argued "that the individual had a current capacity to perform the job, and thus was a qualified handicapped individual."

Varo Semiconductor Company Pays $225,000

In the largest Rehabilitation Act settlement to date, Varo Semiconductor agreed to pay $225,000 to 85 applicants allegedly denied employment because they were handicapped. The settlement resolved claims that the company had systematically used its preemployment physical examinations to disqualify applicants on the basis of such conditions as obesity, color blindness, arthritis, hypertension, allergies, and varicose veins. This decision lent support to the Department of Labor's controversial definition of "handicap" as any physically disqualifying factor.

Future of Litigation

We must bear in mind the warning of _Trial_ (February 1981, Association of Trial Lawyers of America, 1050 31st Street, N.W., Washington, D.C.): "[T]he threat of federal intervention" against violators of Section 503 "is a special kind of leverage" and "a tool of uncommon power" in the hands of aggrieved handicapped individuals filing complaints with the Labor Department.

Therefore we must think not only in terms of whether the handicapped applicant suits the job, but whether the job can be altered to suit the handicapped.

Undefined Standards Are Tricky

Although the Rehabilitation Act does consider such factors as "business necessity" and "financial cost and expenses," far more stress is given to the responsibility of the employer to make "reasonable accommodation," whenever possible. Since the standards are not defined and the penalties for violation are severe, every effort must be made to ensure that our preemployment physicals do not screen out handicapped applicants who are otherwise qualified.

SECTION III

Other In-House
Communications

What you send out is a substitute for your being there. It represents you as much as your voice, manner, clothes, and accomplishments. Don't send less than first-class writing.

Writing is not a giant interruption of what you are doing. It is part of it. Whatever field you are in, you have to transmit your ideas and findings to other people. You can't be a professional all by yourself.

Be sure what you send is a quality product. Good business writing—simple, clear, well organized—is good business.

CHAPTER 8

Reports

What Is a Report?

Reports can be defined as a *record* of something:

- what happened or how things
  were (past)
- how things are now (present)
- how things may be or should
  be (future)

Of course, a one-sentence memo or letter could also perform these functions, so we usually use the word "report" to describe a longer, more formal communication that is intended for a larger audience.

Reports have many forms. The classic report is usually three or more pages, divided into sections or chapters, with a cover page describing the contents. Longer reports usually need a table of contents. Other forms of reports include:

studies	briefs
summaries	guidelines
abstracts	job descriptions
prospectuses	performance evaluations
digests	position statements
analyses	public information releases
profiles	feasibility studies
manuals	progress reports
bulletins	audit reports
directives	fiscal reports
information sheets	

Table of Contents

A common characteristic of reports is that they offer some sort of summary of the contents, either a quick list on the opening page or a separate "Table of Contents" page. If your communication is over three pages and covers several different issues that aren't a natural sequence, you should include a formal or informal table of contents.

Why Are Reports So Important?

There is a saying in many fields that "if it's not documented, it didn't happen." Besides being a useful tool, many reports serve as history. If memos are the daily newspapers of business, reports act as the encyclopedias.

Many reports have the same implied uses as memos:

> to persuade
> to justify
> to prove or deny

It's the importance of a report and the larger audience for it that turn many of us into quivering wrecks when we sit down to write one.

Hiding the Body

Reports are noted for their ability to hide unpleasant things. A report is frequently a justification of something we have been doing or a criticism of what others have been doing. The stakes are high. A "good" report can bring prestige, promotions, and praise. A "bad" report can have serious consequences.

No wonder reports have a reputation for being the most abused form of business writing. Like the Hollywood star who will only be photographed from certain angles, we all know how we want to look to others. A talented writer can hide almost anything temporarily. Subtleties of structure, emphasis, and vocabulary can conceal facts. Statistics can be juggled to show almost anything. Consider one report that stated:

> *The rate of turnover increase in our department has dropped 5%*

when the turnover rate had actually gone up. Or the National Aeronautics and Space Administration report that called the bodies of the Challenger astronauts "recovered components" and their coffins "crew transfer containers."

When the government itself uses euphemisms like "peremptory retaliations" for attacks and "neutralizing" for killing, it is hard to fault business reports that say "negative advancements" when they mean employee demotions and "having a substantial negative net worth" when they mean imminent bankruptcy.

Whenever you are tempted to write this way, just remember Abraham Lincoln's quote about whom you can fool and when and how often.

Reading and Writing Double Talk

Reading a report written in double talk requires all your investigative skills. As you read, try underlining the key points, either mentally or with a pencil, as we have been doing in this book. When your key points don't match the author's, figure out why.

Here's a gem from a 1985 report by the board of education in Ann Arbor, Michigan:

> The purpose of the articulation agreement is to provide a mechanism which will enable vocational-occupational programs at the secondary and post-secondary levels to interface, thereby granting equivalency college credit to students for identified task competencies achieved in secondary programs.

Want to try putting that in English? Here's a possibility: Some high school vocational students, like those enrolled in auto mechanics, carpentry, and other trades, will now be able to get college credit for some high school classes.

What about writing double talk? That's strictly up to you. But writing a report that is confusing, hard to read, or open to misinterpretation should be a *political choice*, not a bad habit. You may choose to write like this, but you shouldn't do it accidentally.

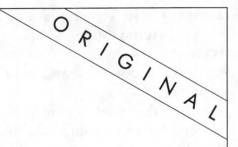

TO: Henry Powers

FROM: Alex Frail

DATE: April 1, 1998

SUBJECT: HAZARDOUS CONDITIONS IN MANUFACTURING AREA

On February 12, I made a tour of the Manufacturing area, and, at that time, found only one aisle that was actually blocked to the extent a janitor's cart could not be pushed through.

Another tour was made on February 16, and all main aisles were clear with the exception of areas located under the ten-ton crane and inside the large shipping door. Of course, there was a lot of shipping activity going on and so it was to be expected, if not desirable.

There is an area that causes problems sporadically in the aisles outside of Department's Polyurethane Room.

It is my understanding that when a machine is being worked on and there is no storage room left inside the Polyurethane Room for the large containers of polyurethane, an area next to the aisle outside the Polyurethane Room has been allocated as a holding space for this polyurethane.

The problem is that Manufacturing has two pallets of parts (awaiting some long-range disposition) that are taking this allocated space, thereby causing an overflow into the aisle under certain conditions.

I spoke to Manufacturing and they said there is no place to move these two pallets in their area.

On these tours, I certainly didn't see the conditions described in the memo dated February 10.

One does see carts and some equipment on wheels taking up approximately twenty-five percent of the aisle's width, but in approximately eighty percent of the cases, there is still room for the janitor's trash cart. However, given the tight quarters Manufacturing has been allocated, I see no way we can disallow rolling stock temporarily parked on edges of aisles.

WHAT TO DO

Yet another once-upon-a-time memo. The reader wants to know "Do we have hazardous conditions?" The writer is taking the reader on a long, roundabout tour. Instead of sounding efficient and meticulous, the writer sounds fussy and self-conscious, possibly unsure of his conclusions.

1. Find the sentence that contains the writer's conclusion and underline it.

2. The writer is responding to an inquiry by the reader. Is he offering only information? Which box would you check?
   [ ] action   [ ] decision   [ ] information

3. Can you find a sentence that contains the writer's recommendation? If so, underline it.

ORIGINAL

TO: Henry Powers

FROM: Alex Frail

DATE: April 1, 1998

SUBJECT: HAZARDOUS CONDITIONS IN MANUFACTURING AREA

On February 12, I made a tour of the Manufacturing area, and, at that time, found only one aisle that was actually blocked to the extent a janitor's cart could not be pushed through.

Another tour was made on February 16, and all main aisles were clear with the exception of areas located under the ten-ton crane and inside the large shipping door. Of course, there was a lot of shipping activity going on and so it was to be expected, if not desirable.

There is an area that causes problems sporadically in the aisles outside of Department's Polyurethane Room.

It is my understanding that when a machine is being worked on and there is no storage room left inside the Polyurethane Room for the large containers of polyurethane, an area next to the aisle outside the Polyurethane Room has been allocated as a holding space for this polyurethane.

The problem is that Manufacturing has two pallets of parts (awaiting some long-range disposition) that are taking this allocated space, thereby causing an overflow into the aisle under certain conditions.

I spoke to Manufacturing and they said there is no place to move these two pallets in their area.

On these tours, I certainly didn't see the conditions described in the memo dated February 10.

One does see carts and some equipment on wheels taking up approximately twenty-five percent of the aisle's width, but in approximately eighty percent of the cases, there is still room for the janitor's trash cart. However, given the tight quarters Manufacturing has been allocated, I see no way we can disallow rolling stock temporarily parked on edges of aisles.

WHAT WE DID

ANSWERS

1. The sentence that contains the writer's conclusion is in paragraph seven: "I certainly didn't see the [hazardous] conditions described in the memo dated February 10."

2. The writer is responding to an inquiry from the reader by offering some solutions to a perceived problem. He should check "decision."

   Avoid checking more than one box unless the contents of a memo cover several separate issues. Presumably all memos contain information. Check "information" only if the principal reason for writing is to give useful background.

3. The sentence that contains the writer's recommendation does not exist in the original memo. It is *implied* by paragraph six: "there is no place to move these two pallets in their area." The writer seems to be hinting that moving the pallets of parts to some other area would alleviate the crowding. In our rewrite, the writer stops hinting and says straight out that moving the pallets is one option to solve the reader's perceived problem. He goes further and recommends a place to move them.

• • • •

OUR REWRITE

SUBJECT CHANGED FROM   Hazardous Conditions in Manufacturing Area

TO   Inspection of Manufacturing Area

TO: Henry Powers, Plant Operations   DATE: April 1, 1998

FROM: Alex Frail

SUBJECT: Inspection of Manufacturing Area

FOR: [ ] action   [X] decision   [ ] information

I've inspected the manufacturing area on two occasions and did not find aisle blockages that were a safety hazard.

There is a minor problem that can be solved by your allocating ___ square feet of storage to Manufacturing. They can then move two pallets of parts that are permanently stored in the aisle outside the department's Polyurethane Room.

I recommend the parts be moved to _____.

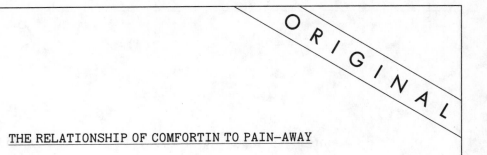

<u>THE RELATIONSHIP OF COMFORTIN TO PAIN—AWAY</u>

COMFORTIN was developed specifically for rapid analgesia. It is chemically unique from PAIN—AWAY and dissolves in the stomach rather than the small intestine. Therefore it is absorbed faster into the blood stream and attains higher peak plasma levels than PAIN—AWAY. These features are desirable in acute pain states where fast, effective pain relief are primary goals.

The analgesic activity of COMFORTIN occurs rapidly. The package insert mentions pain relief within 1 hour. In clinical trials with COMFORTIN, however, onset of analgesia has been reported in as early as 20 minutes.

For chronic, rheumatic inflammatory diseases such as rheumatoid and osteoarthritis, the speed of analgesic onset is generally not crucial. This has been confirmed in a market research survey which showed that physicians treating long—term patients considered drug efficacy a more significant feature than speed of relief.

PAIN—AWAY has years of therapeutic efficacy in relieving the symptoms of arthritis with a high level of safety. It is therefore the appropriate product for the management of this chronic long—term disease.

It is the naproxen anion that is the active component in both COMFORTIN and PAIN—AWAY. COMFORTIN dissociates in the stomach into sodium ions and naproxen anions. Therefore, when the stomach empties into the small intestine, it is the naproxen anion that is absorbed, metabolized,

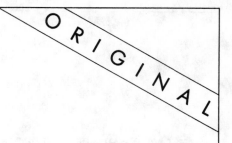

RELATIONSHIP OF COMFORTIN TO PAIN—AWAY—2

utilized, and excreted. Physicians who currently use or are aware of the safe, effective use of PAIN—AWAY view this connection positively.

Efficacy data obtained using naproxen in analgesia studies provides additional support for the analgesic action of COMFORTIN. For example, according to the AMA Drug Evaluations (1990 ed., p. 824), "the analgesic effectiveness of 400 mg of naproxen was greater than that provided by propoxyphene 65 mg in orthopedic pain or aspirin 350 mg with codeine 30 mg in postsurgical dental pain."

In research surveys, fear of unknown side effects often associated with a new drug was reduced following disclosure of the COMFORTIN/PAIN—AWAY link. The credibility of COMFORTIN as being nonaddictive was also strengthened.

The management of chronic conditions such as arthritis are complicated by various social, psychological, and economic problems. Likewise, physician attitudes toward the treatment of acute and chronic pain differ. By providing both COMFORTIN and PAIN—AWAY, physicians are afforded two different products for these two distinct pain states.

Patient perceptions also support the value of having two separate products with distinct physical characteristics for acute and chronic conditions. The patient who has been given blue tablets called "COMFORTIN" for dysmenorrhea, postpartum pain, or a backache

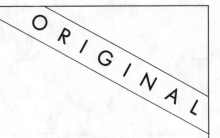

<u>RELATIONSHIP OF COMFORTIN TO PAIN—AWAY—3</u>

might be reluctant to accept this same product should a chronic disease like rheumatoid arthritis or osteoarthritis develop.

In accordance with the suggested clinical uses for COMFORTIN and PAIN—AWAY tablets, suitable dosage schedules were developed during clinical trials. The 550 mg loading dose followed by 275 mg every 6 to 8 hours for COMFORTIN is the dosage required to achieve the analgesic effect necessary for the control of acute pain.

PAIN—AWAY, administered 250, 375, or 500 mg b.i.d. is appropriate for the long—term management of arthritis. While b.i.d. dosage is an excellent compliance feature for treating chronic conditions, patients with acute pain seldom have a compliance problem.

WHAT TO DO

The heading "The Relationship of COMFORTIN to PAIN-AWAY" suggests that this report compares two pain relief products.

1. Put a "C" next to each statement in the original that describes a way that COMFORTIN is superior to PAIN-AWAY.

2. Put a "P" next to each statement in the original that describes a way that PAIN-AWAY is superior to COMFORTIN.

3. Put an "S" next to each statement that describes how the two products are similar.

4. Put a "D" next to each statement that describes how the two products are different.

5. Write a brief overview of the two products here.

THE RELATIONSHIP OF COMFORTIN TO PAIN-AWAY

COMFORTIN was developed specifically for rapid analgesia. It is chemically unique from PAIN-AWAY and dissolves in the stomach rather than the small intestine. Therefore it is absorbed faster into the blood stream and attains higher peak plasma levels than PAIN-AWAY. These features are desirable in acute pain states where fast, effective pain relief are primary goals.

The analgesic activity of COMFORTIN occurs rapidly. The package insert mentions pain relief within 1 hour. In clinical trials with COMFORTIN, however, onset of analgesia has been reported in as early as 20 minutes.

For chronic, rheumatic inflammatory diseases such as rheumatoid and osteoarthritis, the speed of analgesic onset is generally not crucial. This has been confirmed in a market research survey which showed that physicians treating long-term patients considered drug efficacy a more significant feature than speed of relief.

PAIN-AWAY has years of therapeutic efficacy in relieving the symptoms of arthritis with a high level of safety. It is therefore the appropriate product for the management of this chronic long-term disease.

It is the naproxen anion that is the active component in both COMFORTIN and PAIN-AWAY. COMFORTIN dissociates in the stomach into sodium ions and naproxen anions. Therefore, when the stomach empties into the small intestine, it is the naproxen anion that is absorbed, metabolized.

RELATIONSHIP OF COMFORTIN TO PAIN-AWAY—2

utilized, and excreted. Physicians who currently use or are aware of the safe, effective use of PAIN-AWAY view this connection positively.

Efficacy data obtained using naproxen in analgesia studies provides additional support for the analgesic action of COMFORTIN. For example, according to the AMA Drug Evaluations (1990 ed., p. 824), "the analgesic effectiveness of 400 mg of naproxen was greater than that provided by propoxyphene 65 mg in orthopedic pain or aspirin 350 mg with codeine 30 mg in postsurgical dental pain."

In research surveys, fear of unknown side effects often associated with a new drug was reduced following disclosure of the COMFORTIN/PAIN-AWAY link. The credibility of COMFORTIN as being nonaddictive was also strengthened.

The management of chronic conditions such as arthritis are complicated by various social, psychological, and economic problems. Likewise, physician attitudes toward the treatment of acute and chronic pain differ. By providing both COMFORTIN and PAIN-AWAY, physicians are afforded two different products for these two distinct pain states.

Patient perceptions also support the value of having two separate products with distinct physical characteristics for acute and chronic conditions. The patient who has been given blue tablets called "COMFORTIN" for dysmenorrhea, postpartum pain, or a backache

RELATIONSHIP OF COMFORTIN TO PAIN-AWAY—3

might be reluctant to accept this same product should a chronic disease like rheumatoid arthritis or osteoarthritis develop.

In accordance with the suggested clinical uses for COMFORTIN and PAIN-AWAY tablets, suitable dosage schedules were developed during clinical trials. The 550 mg loading dose followed by 275 mg every 6 to 8 hours for COMFORTIN is the dosage required to achieve the analgesic effect necessary for the control of acute pain.

PAIN-AWAY, administered 250, 375, or 500 mg b.i.d. is appropriate for the long-term management of arthritis. While b.i.d. dosage is an excellent compliance feature for treating chronic conditions, patients with acute pain seldom have a compliance problem.

ANSWERS

1. The ways that COMFORTIN is superior to PAIN-AWAY are described in the rewrite under the heading "Advantages of COMFORTIN."

2. The ways that PAIN-AWAY is superior to COMFORTIN are described in the rewrite under the heading "Advantages of PAIN-AWAY."

3. Similarities of the two products are described under "Similarities."

4. Differences are described under "Differences."

5. For a brief overview, see the first section of our Rewrite.

•   •   •   •   •

OUR REWRITE

HEADINGS, headings, headings! They help the reader, but they also help the writer. As soon as you write a heading, you notice what information does and *does not* belong under it.

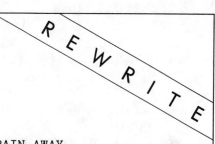

THE RELATIONSHIP OF COMFORTIN TO PAIN-AWAY

COMFORTIN was developed specifically for rapid analgesia and is an alternative to PAIN-AWAY. The key features of the two analgesics are:

COMFORTIN—rapid, effective pain relief for acute pain stages

PAIN-AWAY—long-term efficacy for chronic, rheumatic inflammatory diseases

Advantages of COMFORTIN

COMFORTIN acts rapidly. In clinical trials, onset of analgesia has been reported in as early as 20 minutes. The package insert mentions pain relief within one hour.

Advantages of PAIN-AWAY

A market research survey showed that physicians treating long-term patients considered drug efficacy a more significant feature than speed of relief. PAIN-AWAY, with a record of years of safety and effectiveness in relieving the symptoms of arthritis, is therefore the appropriate product for the management of this chronic, long-term disease.

Similarities

Naproxen anion is the active ingredient of both, but COMFORTIN is chemically unique.

According to the AMA Drug Evaluations (1990 edition, p. 824), "the analgesic effectiveness of 400 mg of naproxen [in COMFORTIN] was greater than that provided by propoxyphene 65 mg in orthopedic pain or aspirin 350 mg with codeine 30 mg in post-surgical dental pain."

Differences

PAIN-AWAY dissociates in the small intestine and is absorbed by the large intestine, while COMFORTIN dissociates in the stomach and is absorbed in the small intestine.

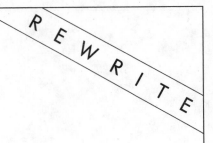

RELATIONSHIP OF COMFORTIN TO PAIN—AWAY—2

Doctor Response

In research surveys, doctors expressed less fear of the unknown side effects often associated with a new drug after they learned of the COMFORTIN/PAIN—AWAY link. The credibility of COMFORTIN as being nonaddictive was also strengthened.

Importance of Offering Both Products

Physician attitudes toward the treatment of acute and chronic pain differ and the management of chronic conditions such as arthritis is complicated by various social, psychological, and economic problems. By providing both COMFORTIN and PAIN—AWAY, we offer the physician a choice.

Also the patient who has been given blue tablets called PAIN—AWAY for dysmenorrhea, postpartum pain, or a backache might be reluctant to accept this same product for a chronic disease like rheumatoid arthritis or osteoarthritis.

Dosages

The following dosage schedules were developed during clinical trials, based on suggested clinical uses.

COMFORTIN: 550 mg loading dose, followed by 275 mg every 6 to 8 hours for acute pain.

PAIN—AWAY: 250, 375, or 500 mg b.i.d., appropriate for the long—term management of arthritis. (While b.i.d. dosage is an excellent compliance feature for treating chronic conditions, patients with acute pain seldom have a compliance problem.)

WHY BOTHER?

Bad writing should be a political choice, not a habit. Sending confusing, hard-to-read communications is good when you want to hide something, but bad when you really want to communicate and get action.

Unintentional bad writing costs energy, time, and money—and can even destroy a good reputation. It's self-defeating. It's ineffective and it's unnecessary. Use the techniques in this book until good business writing becomes a habit.

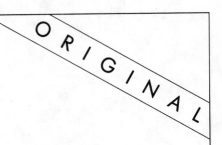

TO: Samuel Foley

FROM: Carl Eckert

DATE: June 24, 1999

SUBJECT: Change in Achievement Level

Don has improved his work performance since his last review 6 months ago. His quality has been excellent with NO REJECTIONS. He has been averaging 130% above parts plant standards.

I've found that he needs little supervision when running the Rogers automatic chuckers. He works well with all coworkers and his supervisor, and is always willing to work overtime when needed.

I am recommending that we change Don Rhodes's merit rating from "M" to "E" with a 3% increase in salary. This will mean a change in his hourly rate to $__ per hour, effective July 9, 1999.

WHAT TO DO

1. Make the subject "Change in Achievement Level" more specific. Write your suggestion here.

2. Why is the reader reading?
   [ ] action   [ ] decision   [ ] information

3. Circle the purpose of this memo—the recommendation.

4. Put a check next to each support for the recommendation.

5. Write a heading for the reasons for the recommendation.

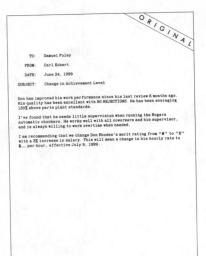

TO: Samuel Foley

FROM: Carl Eckert

DATE: June 24, 1999

SUBJECT: Change in Achievement Level

Don has improved his work performance since his last review 6 months ago. His quality has been excellent with NO REJECTIONS. He has been averaging 130% above parts plant standards.

I've found that he needs little supervision when running the Rogers automatic chuckers. He works well with all coworkers and his supervisor, and is always willing to work overtime when needed.

I am recommending that we change Don Rhodes's merit rating from "M" to "E" with a 3% increase in salary. This will mean a change in his hourly rate to $____ per hour, effective July 9, 1999.

ANSWERS

1. We have changed the subject from:
    Change in Achievement Level
    to
    Change in Achievement Level for Don Rhodes

2. Probably the reader is being asked to decide whether or not to change Don's achievement level. Check "decision."

3. The purpose is in the last paragraph.

4. The areas of accountability listed are:

    > Don has <u>improved his work performance</u> since his last review 6 months ago. His <u>quality has been excellent with NO REJECTIONS</u>. He has been <u>averaging 130% above parts plant standards</u>.
    >
    > I've found that he <u>needs little supervision when running the Rogers automatic chuckers</u>. He <u>works well with all coworkers and his supervisor</u>, and is <u>always willing to work overtime when needed</u>.

    These supports suggest the subheads in the rewrite:

    > Quality
    > Quantity
    > Job knowledge
    > Work habits
    > Dependability

5. We have used the heading "Reasons for Recommendation" but other headings would be equally appropriate:

    > Background
    > Supports
    > Don's Good Work

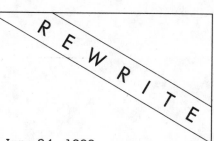

TO: Samuel Foley   DATE: June 24, 1999

FROM: Carl Eckert

SUBJECT: Change in Achievement Level for Don Rhodes

FOR: [ ] action   [X] decision   [ ] information

I am recommending that we change Don Rhodes's merit rating from "M" to "E" with a 3% increase in salary. This will change his hourly rate to $__ per hour, effective July 9, 1999.

Reasons for Recommendation

Don has improved his work performance since his last review 6 months ago and exceeds our requirements in most areas of accountability:

Quality: Don's quality has been excellent with NO REJECTIONS.

Quantity: He has been averaging 130% above parts plant standards.

Job knowledge: needs little supervision when running the Rogers automatic chuckers.

Work habits: works well with all coworkers and his supervisor.

Dependability: always willing to work overtime when needed.

CHAPTER 9

Proposals

A proposal can be a two-hundred-page formal bid for a multimillion dollar project, or it can be a brief note asking for a new typewriter ribbon. In either case, the writer is asking the reader to decide in favor of something the writer wants. The writer is asking for a *decision*.

All proposals require the same things:

1. *overview*—a clear opening statement of what is proposed, what the reader is being asked to approve

2. *description* of what is proposed

3. *supports* for the request, including:
   necessity of proposed action (legal, ethical, financial)
   benefits to reader (how the reader will gain by agreeing with the proposal)
   facts, history, background about the situation

Always begin with a clear opening statement of what is being proposed. Then provide the description. Here's where you have to decide what the reader needs to know at this stage.

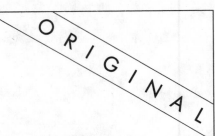

TO:	Nicholas Fouquet	DATE:	September 29, 1996
FROM:	Paul Pellison	cc:	Madeleine de Scudery
RE:	Salary Adjustments		

Having completed one year in Spector's Mailroom, I would like to discuss how the responsibilities of the Mailroom have grown during that time. Spector has grown in such a way that the volume of input to the Mailroom has increased substantially, causing a major growth in the responsibilities of the two individuals employed to run the Mailroom.

The extent of Spector's high-volume/deadline mailings, shippings, and high-volume copying requiring customized attention has increased dramatically. I can easily produce records which demonstrate these facts. Additionally, I am responsible for supervising a Mailroom Assistant, who changes every three months. Lastly, I balance a position of "office boy," involving <u>all</u> miscellaneous duties, from kitchen cleanup to moving furniture to, in the near future, switchboard relief.

Managing all this is possible through experiencing Spector's growth day by day. And my job has been challenging. The only thing I find inadequate is my salary. My Assistant's salary is also inadequate, and is the source of why it is difficult to keep any one person in that position.

Spector's Mailroom runs on a budget that I believe is in excess of $500,000, and is supporting groups such as the Workshop Division, which recently boasted completion of $1,000,000 in business through August's end. The work completed in the Mailroom has been essential to their, and Spector's, success.

I would like to request a salary adjustment which would reflect the responsibility of these kinds of figures. I think a salary of $20,000 per year for the Mailroom Supervisor, and $15,000 for his Assistant would fairly reflect the volume and responsibility carried by each position.

WHAT TO DO

Asking for a raise is actually making a proposal. You are offering reasons why the reader will want to decide in your favor.

1. Does the subject "Salary Adjustments" tell the reader why he is reading?

2. Does the opening paragraph tell the reader why he is reading? Find the purpose of the memo and underline it.

3. Put a check next to the supports for the request.

4. Are there any other supports that the writer could supply that might strengthen his request? List some below.

TO: Nicholas Fouquet   DATE: September 29, 1996

FROM: Paul Pellison   cc: Madeleine de Scudery

RE: Salary Adjustments

Having completed one year in Spector's Mailroom, I would like to discuss how the responsibilities of the Mailroom have grown during that time. Spector has grown in such a way that the volume of input to the Mailroom has increased substantially, causing a major growth in the responsibilities of the two individuals employed to run the Mailroom.

The extent of Spector's high-volume/deadline mailings, shippings, and high-volume copying requiring customized attention has increased dramatically. I can easily produce records which demonstrate these facts. Additionally, I am responsible for supervising a Mailroom Assistant, who changes every three months. Lastly, I balance a position of "office boy," involving all miscellaneous duties, from kitchen cleanup to moving furniture to, in the near future, switchboard relief.

Managing all this is possible through experiencing Spector's growth day by day. And my job has been challenging. The only thing I find inadequate is my salary. My Assistant's salary is also inadequate, and is the source of why it is difficult to keep any one person in that position.

Spector's Mailroom runs on a budget that I believe is in excess of $500,000, and is supporting groups such as the Workshop Division, which recently boasted completion of $1,000,000 in business through August's end. The work completed in the Mailroom has been essential to their, and Spector's, success.

I would like to request a salary adjustment which would reflect the responsibility of these kinds of figures. I think a salary of $20,000 per year for the Mailroom Supervisor, and $15,000 for his Assistant would fairly reflect the volume and responsibility carried by each position.

ANSWERS

1. The subject "Salary Adjustments" doesn't tell the reader why he is reading. What kind of adjustments? Whose salary?

2. The opening paragraph doesn't directly tell the reader why he is reading. The purpose—the request for two salary adjustments—is found in paragraph five.

3. Supports include:
   a. volume of input has increased substantially
   b. extent of high-volume/deadline copying has increased dramatically
   c. "I can easily produce records which demonstrate these facts"
   d. major growth in the responsibilities of two individuals . . .
   e. assistant changes every three months
   f. miscellaneous duties
   g. budget in excess of $500,000
   h. Workshop Division completed $1 million in business; mailroom essential to their success

4. Additional supports:
   a. documentation and statistics on work increases
   b. comparative salaries at other companies

•   •   •   •   •

OUR REWRITE

SUBJECT CHANGED FROM   Salary Adjustments

TO   Request for Mailroom Salary Increases

REWRITE starts with the request for a raise.

SUPPORTS should be itemized in order of effectiveness. Delete general comments which cannot be readily supported.

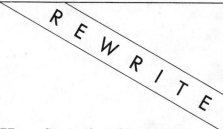

TO: Nicholas Fouquet   DATE: September 29, 1996

FROM: Paul Pellison   CC: Madeleine de Scudery

SUBJECT: Request for Mailroom Salary Increases

FOR: [ ] action   [X] decision   [ ] information

I request a salary increase to $20,000 for myself as Mailroom Supervisor, and to $15,000 for my assistant, based on increased work load, expanded duties, and current competitive salaries.

Increased Work Load

In the year that I have been in Spector's mailroom, my assistant and I have successfully handled the following work increases:

	Aug. 1995	Aug. 1996
Average pieces of mail per day	0000	0000
Average copies made per day	0000	0000
Number of customized jobs	000	000

Expanded Duties

My added duties now include all miscellaneous office jobs such as furniture moving, kitchen cleanup, and, starting next week, switchboard relief.

Competitive Salaries Are Higher

There is high turnover in the Mailroom Assistant position, largely because of the low salary offered as compared to the heavy work load. I have trained three new assistants in the last year. According to the Sunday, September 26, Spectorville News and several employment agencies I contacted, current starting salaries are:

	Mailroom Supervisor	Mailroom Assistant
Newspaper ads	$00,000–$00,000	$00,000–$00,000
Agencies	$00,000–$00,000	$00,000–$00,000

Importance of Mailroom

Spector's mailroom runs on a budget of over $500,000 and supports groups like the Workshop Division which recently boasted completion of $1 million in business through the end of August. The mailroom has been essential to their success and Spector's.

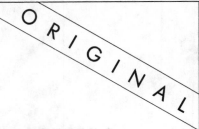

Proposed: a system of providing training in the field for the U.S. network of SPECTOR stores.

HISTORY

The first training provided in the field has been "Controlling the Retail Sale," the fundamental sales training course for SPECTOR sales staff, developed by WITraining. This training was announced at the 1998 International Conference and presented beginning in September.

Scheduling for the first year was intended to get the new program to every franchise at least once.

Since September 1998, and through November 1999, this course will be taught 92 times. Through the first week in September 1999, 1,007 participants have successfully completed the course.

A total of eighteen trainings will have been presented outside of the United States: SPECTOR Japan = 1; SPECTOR Paris = 1; SPECTOR Australia = 4; SPECTOR Europe = 4; and SPECTOR Canada = 8.

This was accomplished with three full-time sales trainers until September 1999, when we are adding a fourth, plus one "back up" or part-time trainer.

The first year's success should be and is attributed to Renee Wu, Training Manager, and her ability to train and manage the trainers.

ANALYSIS

While we did get around to key areas in the first year, we were not able to present the course on a regular basis in areas with new franchises and stores having new employees.

The concept of "training territories" is to provide a system of offering field training consistently and geographically convenient to all SPECTOR stores. While the only training currently given in the field is the sales training, this system is adaptable for future use.

We further propose that this system be announced to SPECTOR vendors, who may wish to follow up our sales training with product training.

The training territories (see Exhibit A) were designed based on the current locations of SPECTOR stores and logical choices for training locations.

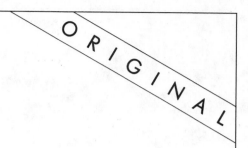

Page 2

We proposed that training be scheduled in each of the twenty—six territories each quarter and delivered contingent on desire of franchises in the territory. In other words, should we discover that a territory does not require a training in a quarter, that class will be dropped from that quarter's schedule.

We believe it a better approach to have store owners and managers request that we postpone our trip, rather than have to call and ask when we will be able to get around to them.

This proposal includes suggested locations for classes in each territory. These suggestions are based on geography, past history, and optimum hotel and transportation services. Of course, they are subject to revision, based on input from franchise owners in the territory.

Four sales trainers, presenting two to three trainings per month each, will adequately provide 26 trainings per quarter with ease.

SPECTOR International has requested assistance with sales training in English—speaking areas for at least the first two quarters of 2000. We believe that we can provide six International trainings per quarter, beyond serving the sales training needs of the 98 domestic territories.

When not in the field, sales trainers will study the market statistics in each territory, and stay abreast of product trends in the industry.

The Sales Training Coordinator will maintain regular contact with all franchises to determine that training is available as needed.

SUMMARY

This proposal is for staffing the Training Programs Department with trainers, who will be responsible for the professional and effective delivery of training programs to SPECTOR managers, sales personnel and Corporate staff.

Given the program development plans of the Training Department through 2000, we are proposing three groups of trainers.

First group is <u>sales trainers</u>. Based on a plan for territorial field sales training (see separate proposal), we believe that four trainers, delivering 2—3 trainings per month will be able to serve the United States SPECTOR stores on a consistent and regular basis. A Senior Sales Trainer will supervise this effort.

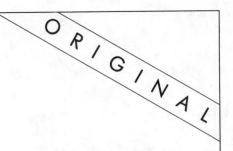

Second trainer group is <u>manager trainers</u>. They will be responsible for delivery of the eventual six week cycle of fundamental training for new store managers. Each of the four will have a particular area of expertise: management, operations, financial and sales/marketing. Again, a Senior Francise Manager will oversee the efforts of this group.

Third group is <u>corporate trainers</u>. This group will be responsible for providing quality training in management and other skills to the rapidly growing corporation employee population.

Long-range plans include cross-training of all groups, providing for job enrichment and/or enlargement.

All trainers will be responsible for staying current on events related to 1) SPECTOR, 2) the SPECTOR network of retail stores, 3) the industry and market, and 4) the field of training.

Job descriptions, projected dates of hire and proposed salaries attached.

SUMMARY

To meet performance objectives through the third quarter of 2000, Training Coordination must be staffed appropriately.

The purpose of Training Coordination is to arrange for and ensure the professional production of all SPECTOR training courses, for store managers, store salespeople, and corporate staff.

The proposed staffing plan is for eleven (11) positions. Five (5) of these positions are required for now (September 1999) through December 1999. Two (2) will be added in the first quarter of 2000. The other four (4) positions are tentatively scheduled through the second and third quarters of 2000 and are subject to actual need, which will be clarified over the next six months.

Job descriptions have been written for all but two of the proposed positions (the two least defined needs). These descriptions reflect a requirement for professional skills, experience and responsibilities. Salary range suggestions have been proposed in this light.

The Training Coordination unit has been planned as the "bedrock" function of the Training Department. It must be staffed and organized to support training programs for 400 U.S. stores through 1999, plus temporary training provided to International and 1,000 U.S. stores through 2000. In addition, we will coordinate training for corporate staff, 500+ as of September 1, 1999.

WHAT TO DO

This original has four headings:

> History
> Analysis
> Summary
> Summary
> (Yes, *two* summaries!)

1. Start by putting a check next to the actions that the writer is proposing for Spector.

2. Identify background information (history) by writing a "B" next to it.

3. Write possible headings for this report.

4. Which of the sections you identified above should come first? Number the sections in their logical order of importance.

ORIGINAL

Proposed: a system of providing training in the field for the U.S. network of SPECTOR stores.

HISTORY

The first training provided in the field has been "Controlling the Retail Sale," the fundamental sales training course for SPECTOR sales staff, developed by WITraining. This training was announced at the 1998 International Conference and presented beginning in September.
Scheduling for the first year was intended to get the new program to every franchise at least once.
Since September 1998, and through November 1999, this course will be taught 92 times. Through the first week in September 1999, 1,007 participants have successfully completed the course.
A total of eighteen trainings will have been presented outside of the United States: SPECTOR Japan = 1; SPECTOR Paris = 1; SPECTOR Australia = 4; SPECTOR Europe = 4; and SPECTOR Canada = 8.
This was accomplished with three full-time sales trainers until September 1999, when we are adding a fourth, plus one "back up" or part-time trainer.
The first year's success should be and is attributed to Renee Wu, Training Manager, and her ability to train and manage the trainers.

ANALYSIS

While we did get around to key areas in the first year, we were not able to present the course on a regular basis in areas with new franchises and stores having new employees.
The concept of "training territories" is to provide a system of offering field training consistently and geographically convenient to all SPECTOR stores. While the only training currently given in the field is the sales training, this system is adaptable for future use.
We further propose that this system be announced to SPECTOR vendors, who may wish to follow up our sales training with product training.
The training territories (see Exhibit A) were designed based on the current locations of SPECTOR stores and logical choices for training locations.

Page 2

We proposed that training be scheduled in each of the twenty-six territories each quarter and delivered contingent of desire of franchises in the territory. In other words, should we discover that a territory does not require a training in a quarter, that class will be dropped from that quarter's schedule.
We believe it a better approach to have store owners and managers request that we postpone our trip, rather than have to call and ask when we will be able to get around to them.
This proposal includes suggested locations for classes in each territory. These suggestions are based on geography, past history, and optimum hotel and transportation services. Of course, they are subject to revision, based on input from franchise owners in the territory.
Four sales trainers, presenting two to three trainings each month each, will adequately provide 26 trainings per quarter with ease.
SPECTOR International has requested assistance with sales training in English-speaking areas for at least the first two quarters of 2000. We believe that we can provide six International trainings per quarter, beyond serving the sales training needs of the 98 domestic territories.
When not in the field, sales trainers will study the market statistics in each territory, and stay abreast of product trends in the industry.
The Sales Training Coordinator will maintain regular contact with all franchises to determine that training is available as needed.

SUMMARY

This proposal is for staffing the Training Programs Department with trainers, who will be responsible for the professional and effective delivery of training programs to SPECTOR managers, sales personnel and Corporate staff.
Given the program development plans of the Training Department through 2000, we are proposing three groups of trainers.
First group is sales trainers. Based on a plan for territorial field sales training (see separate proposal), we believe that four trainers, delivering 2-3 trainings per month will be able to serve the United States SPECTOR stores on a consistent and regular basis. A Senior Sales Trainer will supervise this effort.

Page 3

Second trainer group is manager trainers. They will be responsible for delivery of the eventual six week cycle of fundamental training for new store managers. Each of the four will have a particular area of expertise: management, operations, financial and sales/marketing. Again, a Senior Franchise Manager will oversee the efforts of this group.
Third group is corporate trainers. This group will be responsible for providing quality training in management and other skills to the rapidly growing corporation employee population.
Long-range plans include cross-training of all groups, providing for job enrichment and/or enlargement.
All trainers will be responsible for staying current on events related to 1) SPECTOR, 2) the SPECTOR network of retail stores, 3) the industry and market, and 4) the field of training.
Job descriptions, projected dates of hire and proposed salaries attached.

SUMMARY

To meet performance objectives through the third quarter of 2000, Training Coordination must be staffed appropriately.
The purpose of Training Coordination is to arrange for and ensure the professional production of all SPECTOR training courses, for store managers, store salespeople, and corporate staff.
The proposed staffing plan is for eleven (11) positions. Five (5) of these positions are required for now (September 1999) through December 1999. Two (2) will be added in the first quarter of 2000. The other four (4) positions are tentatively scheduled through the second and third quarters of 2000 and are subject to actual need, which will be clarified over the next six months.
Job descriptions have been written for all but two of the proposed positions (the two least defined needs). These descriptions reflect a requirement for professional skills, experience and responsibilities. Salary range suggestions have been proposed in this light.
The Training Coordination unit has been planned as the "bedrock" function of the Training Department. It must be staffed and organized to support training programs for 400 U.S. stores through 1999, plus temporary training provided to International and 1,000 U.S. stores through 2000. In addition, we will coordinate training for corporate staff, 500+ as of September 1, 1999.

ANSWERS

1–2.   Check your answers on the opposite page.

3.   Possible headings:

> Proposed Staffing
> Proposed Training Territories
> Proposed Training Coordination Unit
> Proposed Scheduling
> Proposed Procedures
> Success of First Training Program (background/history)

4.   "Proposed Staffing" should be first, "Success of First Training Program" last. The others can be in any order in between.

• • • •

OUR REWRITE

OVERVIEW: Any report longer than three pages should have a summary, overview, or index on page one. Because of the several attachments, this proposal will be rather hefty and will definitely benefit by an overview page.

ATTACHMENTS: These should be listed at the end of any report if they are not covered in an index.

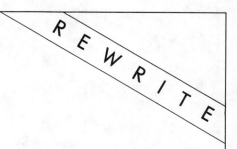

PROPOSAL

A Field Training System for Spector's U.S. Stores

SUMMARY

We propose to:

A. Add and structure staff for Training Programs Department

   Current manpower would increase from four to eleven trainers. These
   trainers would be responsible for the professional and effective
   delivery of training programs to Spector managers, sales personnel,
   and Corporate staff.

B. Set up "training territories"

   These would provide a system for offering consistent field training,
   geographically convenient to all Spector stores. While sales training
   is the only training currently given in the field, this system would be
   adaptable for future needs.

C. Set up Training Coordination Unit

   This would consist of [title], [title], [etc.].

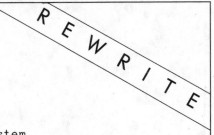

PROPOSAL—Field Training System

Proposed Staffing

To fulfill the program development plans of the Training Department
through the year 2000, we are proposing eleven trainers divided into three
groups. Job descriptions, projected dates of hire, and proposed salaries
are attached.

11 trainer positions
- 5 required for now (September 1999) through December 1999
- 2 to be added in the first quarter of 2000
- 4 tentatively scheduled through the second and third quarters of 2000
  and subject to actual need, which will be clarified over the next six
  months.

3 trainer groups
- 4 SALES TRAINERS—Based on a plan for territorial field sales training
  (see separate proposal), we believe that four sales trainers, each
  presenting two to three trainings per month, would adequately provide
  26 U.S. trainings and 6 international trainings per quarter. The
  international trainings are in response to a request from Spector
  International for assistance in English-speaking areas for at least
  the first two quarters of 2000. A senior sales trainer would supervise
  this group.
- 4 MANAGER TRAINERS—These trainers would be responsible for delivering
  the eventual six-week cycle of fundamental training for new store
  managers. Each of the four would have a particular area of expertise:

  > Management
  > Operations
  > Financial
  > Sales/Marketing

  A senior franchise trainer would oversee this group.

- 3 CORPORATE TRAINERS—This group would be responsible for providing
  quality training in management and other skills to the rapidly growing
  corporate employee population.

PROPOSAL—Field Training System
Page 2

<u>Additional Trainer Responsibilities</u>
When not in the field, sales trainers would study the market statistics in
each territory and stay abreast of product trends in the industry. All
trainers would be responsible for staying current on events related to:
- Spector Corporation
- Spector retail network
- the industry and market
- the training field

<u>Proposed Training Territories</u>
The training territories and locations are based on the current locations
of Spector stores. Locations for classes in each territory, based on
geography, past history, and optimum hotel and transportation services,
are attached. They are subject to revision after input from franchise
owners in each territory.

<u>Proposed Training Coordination Unit</u>
This supervisory unit has been planned as the "bedrock" of the Training
Department. It would consist of _____ people:

Training Manager
[Title]
[Title]
[Title]

It must be staffed and organized to support training programs for more than
400 U.S. stores through 1999, plus temporary training provided to
International and 1,000 U.S. stores through 2000. In addition, we would
coordinate training for corporate staff, 500+ as of September 1, 1999.

<u>Proposed Scheduling</u>
We propose that training be scheduled in each of the 26 territories each
quarter, but delivered on an <u>as-needed basis</u>. We believe it is better to
have store owners and managers request that we <u>postpone</u> our trip, rather
than have them call us to schedule a visit.

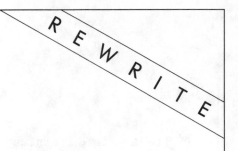

PROPOSAL—Field Training System
Page 3

Proposed Procedures
Long-range plans include cross-training of all groups, providing for job
enrichment and/or enlargement.

We further propose that this system be announced to Spector vendors, who
may wish to follow up our sales training with product training.

Success of First Training Program
"Controlling the Retail Sale" has been the first training provided in the
field. It is a fundamental sales training course developed by WITraining.
    In the U.S.   Between September 1998 and November 1999, this course will
have been taught 92 times. Through the first week of September 1999, 1,007
participants will have successfully completed this course.
    Outside the U.S.   A total of 18 trainings will have been presented:

Spector Japan	1
Spector Paris	1
Spector Australia	4
Spector Europe	4
Spector Canada	8

    Scheduling   for the first year was intended to get the new program to
every franchise at least once. While we did get around to key areas in the
first year, we were not able to present the course on a regular basis in
areas with new franchises and to stores having new employees.
    Staffing   We had three full-time sales trainers through September
1999. A fourth trainer and one "back-up" or part-time trainer are being
added to complete the program.
    Reasons for Success   We owe this first year's success to Renee Wu,
Training Manager, and her ability to train and to manage the trainers.

Attachments: Map of training territories and locations
              Job descriptions
              Projected dates of hire
              Proposed salaries

CHAPTER 10

Minutes

Minutes are one of the most abused forms of inter-office communication. How many times have you found someone's transcribed meeting notes in your in-box, disguised as a memo?

Of course, it's usually important and even legally necessary to chronicle what has happened at a meeting and to keep detailed records of decisions, proposals, and plans—but it's rarely important to send that record to everyone.

MINUTES are for record keeping. They are for your own use.

(Minutes are like exploratory writing.)

MEETING SUMMARIES are for conclusions, decisions, and action plans for others to see.

(Meeting summaries are like crafted writing.)

When you are responsible for the minutes of a meeting, start by writing everything down in chronological order in the traditional way. After the meeting, go back and add appropriate headings as you've already learned to do. This will help you recognize and collect related information from throughout the minutes.

Now decide *who* needs to know and *what* they need to know. In most cases a meeting summary is the most efficient and informative way to share the information with a large audience.

Go back through the minutes and divide what was said into action/decision/information categories. Underline the names of people who have agreed to do something or who will be affected by a decision made at the meeting. Your summary might begin like this:

```
FOR ACTION

    Bernard Farr will work up cost comparisons for
    moving or expanding our Oshkosh facility and
    report his findings at the April 28 meeting.

    All department heads should notify affected
    personnel about the June 12 closing of the main
    headquarters during installation of the new
    phone system. Janet Shore is responsible for
    notifying them about this.

FOR DECISION

    Sam Carpenter, Ruth Gross, and Lynn Belve-
    dere are collecting input and will meet in
    early May to evaluate whether we should ex-
    pand the Oshkosh facility or move to a new lo-
    cation.

FOR INFORMATION

    Home-office shutdown on June 12: We have se-
    lected the phone system, clearly the best in-
    terface with our computers, to replace our
    current obsolete system. The main office will
    be closed one day, Saturday, June 12, while it
    is installed.
```

Another format *may* be more efficient in a special case, for instance:

- by dates of actions—a timetable with the names of acting and affected people clearly highlighted
- by departments, listing their responsibilities or agreed-upon actions first, then current activities and past actions

- by departments or individuals affected
- by types of activity—"Accounting Move," "Personnel Changes," "Nebraska Lawsuit."

Be keenly aware that *content will dictate format*.

At the end of the meeting summary, offer detailed minutes to those who may want them:

> Copies of the minutes can be obtained from Sy Woods, G-1207, ext. 377.

Finally, file the detailed minutes with the meeting summary firmly stapled on top, where it will act as a "table of contents" in the future when someone needs to retrieve specific information about a decision or discussion.

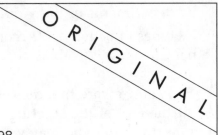

TO: FILE   December 21, 1998

FROM: Maddie Hayes

SUBJECT: December 20th Food Supplement Strategy Group Meeting

The purpose of this memorandum is to provide documentation of the decisions made at the December 20th Food Supplement Strategy Group Meeting.

The objective of the meeting was to organize the group toward meeting its goal of developing the best possible F/S strategic plan by April 1, 1999.

The attached schematic illustrates how the problem was approached. First, because of time constraints within the group, only certain aspects of our current products such as cost minimization, pricing, positioning and advertising will be considered. Instead, the scope of this group will be to develop alternatives which will add directly to the Spector product line.

Specifically, Bert Viola will work on long-range (10–20 years) planning developing alternatives which have the potential for providing products in the next decade. The remainder of the group will concentrate on products and companies Spector would acquire, or new product concepts Spector could develop in the near future. Agnes and David will concentrate on the product positioning area; Frank and Walter, the pricing; and Dennis, promotional.

Meetings will be held every two weeks for the next three months. Each subgroup is responsible for presenting its findings and future plans to the entire strategy group at each meeting. These presentations should be "brainstorming" sessions with input from all group members. Hopefully this format will lead to group consensus regarding the priority of recommended alternatives.

The meetings in January will be January 15 and 29, and every second and fourth Monday in February and March.

cc: F/S Strategy Group

Attachments

WHAT TO DO

This writer has tried to summarize a meeting for a general audience. Let's make it even easier to read.

1. Put a check next to the long-term objective(s).

2. Circle the short-term objective(s) and underline the person(s) responsible.

3. Suggest a clearer way to describe future meetings here.

The original memo reads:

TO: FILE   December 21, 1998

FROM: Maddie Hayes

SUBJECT: December 20th Food Supplement Strategy Group Meeting

The purpose of this memorandum is to provide documentation of the decisions made at the December 20th Food Supplement Strategy Group Meeting.

The objective of the meeting was to organize the group toward meeting its goal of developing the best possible F/S strategic plan by April 1, 1999.

The attached schematic illustrates how the problem was approached. First, because of time constraints within the group, only certain aspects of our current products such as cost minimization, pricing, positioning and advertising will be considered. Instead, the scope of this group will be to develop alternatives which will add directly to the Spector product line.

Specifically, Bert Viola will work on long-range (10–20 years) planning developing alternatives which have the potential for providing products in the next decade. The remainder of the group will concentrate on products and companies Spector would acquire, or new product concepts Spector could develop in the near future. Agnes and David will concentrate on the product positioning area; Frank and Walter, the pricing; and Dennis, promotional.

Meetings will be held every two weeks for the next three months. Each subgroup is responsible for presenting its findings and future plans to the entire strategy group at each meeting. These presentations should be "brainstorming" sessions with input from all group members. Hopefully this format will lead to group consensus regarding the priority of recommended alternatives.

The meetings in January will be January 15 and 29, and every second and fourth Monday in February and March.

cc: F/S Strategy Group

Attachments

ANSWERS

1. The long-term objective is in paragraph two: "to organize the group toward meeting its goal of developing the best possible F/S strategic plan by April 1, 1999."

2. The short-term objectives and those responsible for them are in paragraphs three and four and are presented in chart format in the rewrite under the heading "Responsibilities."

3. A clearer way to describe future meetings appears in the rewrite under the heading "Future Meeting Schedule."

• • • •

OUR REWRITE

FORMAT is changed from a traditional memo to a simpler meeting summary.

ATTACHMENT: The schematic of how the group made decisions is no longer attached. It is an example of "thinking on paper" and probably serves no real purpose for the readers.

ADDITIONAL INFORMATION includes details about time and location of meetings and how to obtain a copy of the complete minutes (presumably along with the handsome schematic about how the attendees approached the problem).

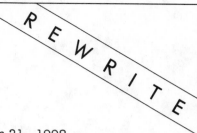

```
TO:        FILE              DATE:   December 21, 1998

FROM:      Maddie Hayes      CC:     F/S Strategy Group

MTG. DATE: December 20, 1998
```

MEETING SUMMARY

Food Supplement Strategy Planning

Objective of Meeting
Preparing marketing plans for new food supplement by April 1.

Decisions
We will limit our focus to cost minimization, pricing, positioning, and advertising.

We will hold regular brainstorming sessions for the next three months to hear reports on products and companies Spector could acquire and on new product concepts that Spector could develop. Input from all group members is expected.

Responsibilities
These people will report on these topics at each meeting:

Bert Viola	Products for the next decade
Agnes Dipesto David Addison	Product positioning
Frank McGillicudy Walter Bishop	Pricing
Dennis Dugan	Promotional strategies

Future Meeting Schedule
We will meet Tuesdays at 10:00 A.M. in room 721 on:

January 15	February 12	March 12
January 29	February 26	March 26

Detailed minutes can be obtained from Bob Bartel, ext. 338.

CHAPTER 11

Statistics

Nothing divides a group faster than laying a page of numbers on the table. Some people will brighten visibly, now having a real handle on the matter being discussed. Others will wilt and slump in their seats, faced with information as cryptic as Minoan Linear B script.

This division in how people respond to numbers can create strong (but erroneous) impressions about the relative intelligence and friendliness of coworkers. If you're one of those whose eyes glaze over when faced with columns of numbers, it will help you to understand that statistics means comparing one number to another. Numbers can only do three things:

> They can go up.
> They can go down.
> They can stay the same.

The drama comes in choosing which numbers to compare with each other and interpreting what the up/down/same means. It's easy to compare numbers in self-serving ways:

"Four out of five dentists we talked to prefer Goo-Goo gum." *(We found four dentists who own Goo-Goo stock.)*

"27 times more effective . . ." *(Than what? Is the comparison valid?)*

"The decline in literacy has increased 7 percent." *(Fewer people can read now than before.)*

When you run across statistics, be sure you're clear about what is being compared to what. Is that comparison valid? Do you agree with the interpretation of those statistics? Is the conclusion accurate?

Number People and Word People

Four hundred years ago it was possible for one bright person to know everything there was to know about physics, mathematics, astronomy, medicine, chemistry, history, geography, and the arts. Since the days of the Renaissance, we've expanded our knowledge of the universe somewhat and we've begun to specialize.

The twentieth century has created two kinds of people who have trouble with business writing:

The Number Person	who is uncomfortable with words and wants a precision that can be numbingly dull and even miss the main point.
The Word Person	who is uncomfortable with numbers and wants a dramatic overview that can be distorting or even misinterpreted.

Knowing how to turn the information provided by numbers into verbal concepts is equally important for the *number person* and the *word person*. Do the exercise in this chapter, as precisely or dramatically as you wish, to strengthen this essential skill.

> Much business writing is boring, some is ineffective, and some is even dangerous. This isn't because the writers are stupid or being deliberately obscure. They are just imitating what they see in their in-box every day. They have rarely been exposed to good business writing.

TO: Paul Collins   DATE: May 6, 1999

FROM: Jill Coogan

SUBJECT: VALENCIA PROJECT VARIANCES

Attached is a summary report of the expenses for the Valencia project. The largest over budget expenses is in the labor expense account, which is $40,915 over budget year-to-date. This variance is due to the addition of a group analyst in January which was not budgeted for. Office supplies equipment is over budget by $23,208 as a result of the purchase of 2 pieces of office equipment which again was not budgeted for. Operating expense, depreciation and occupancy, and metered expenses are all significantly under budget.

Operating expense is under budget by $32,746 primarily due to auto lease expense, which is $19,011 under budget. After further investigation, it was discovered that the Valencia project is only being charged for one company car and it should be charged for two. The remainder of the variance is composed of several small accounts which are under budget.

Depreciation and occupancy is under budget by $18,074 or 43%. The Valencia Project is only being charged for about one-half of the square footage it is budgeted for. Tina Feisty in Plant Facilities is following up on this.

Metered Expenses are under budget by $47,029 or 78%. The majority of this variance is comprised of accounts #225—Fabrication and Services and account #900—Technical Publications. The combined budget for these two accounts is $3,502 year-to-date and both accounts have a zero balance. Account #445—Reproduction Costs In-house is also under budget $7,544.

If you have any questions, please call me.

cc: Shawn Dubin
     Shenandoah Evans
     Demian Clardon

WHAT TO DO

This memo describes an attached summary report. Since the report is already a "summary," the writer could let the report speak for itself. But let's assume that the writer wants to give the reader the highlights of the reports.

1. The writer discusses budget items that fall into two different categories. What are the categories?

   a. _____

   b. _____

   These should be your headings.

2. Go through the memo and mark all items in the "a" category with an *a*. Mark all items in the "b" category with a *b*.

3. Decide what the remaining information (neither *a* nor *b*) does?

   • Offers further explanations of these items? (If so, it should go under the headings.)

   • Offers solutions to a problem? (If so, it probably doesn't deserve its own heading.)

   • Makes a recommendation or proposal? (If so, it requires its own heading.)

   • Offers unrelated information? (If so, it requires its own heading.)

WHAT WE DID

TO: Paul Collins   DATE: May 6, 1999

FROM: Jill Coogan

SUBJECT: VALENCIA PROJECT VARIANCES

Attached is a summary report of the expenses for the Valencia project. The largest over budget expenses is in the labor expense account, which is $40,915 over budget year-to-date. This variance is due to the addition of a group analyst in January which was not budgeted for. Office supplies equipment is over budget by $23,208 as a result of the purchase of 2 pieces of office equipment which again was not budgeted for. Operating expense, depreciation and occupancy, and metered expenses are all significantly under budget.

Operating expense is under budget by $32,746 primarily due to auto lease expense, which is $19,011 under budget. After further investigation, it was discovered that the Valencia project is only being charged for one company car and it should be charged for two. The remainder of the variance is composed of several small accounts which are under budget.

Depreciation and occupancy is under budget by $18,074 or 43%. The Valencia Project is only being charged for about one-half of the square footage it is budgeted for. Tina Feisty in Plant Facilities is following up on this.

Metered Expenses are under budget by $47,029 or 78%. The majority of this variance is comprised of accounts #225—Fabrication and Services and account #900—Technical Publications. The combined budget for these two accounts is $3,502 year-to-date and both accounts have a zero balance. Account #445—Reproduction Costs In-house is also under budget $7,544.

If you have any questions, please call me.

cc: Shawn Dubin
     Shenandoah Evans
     Deaian Clardon

ANSWERS

1.   a.   Over-budget items
     b.   Under-budget items
2.   Over- and under-budget items are listed in the chart of the rewrite.
3.   The remaining information explains the over- and under-budget items, so it is treated as supports on the chart.

•   •   •   •   •

OUR REWRITE

SUBJECT CHANGED FROM   Valencia Project Variances (variances of what?)

TO   Budget Report for Valencia Project

CHART: Use a chart to compare things if it makes it easier to spot the differences and similarities, if it will take up less space, or if it will clarify the information.

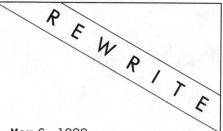

```
        TO:     Paul Collins          DATE:    May 6, 1999

      FROM:     Jill Coogan           CC:      Shawn Dubin
                                               Shenandoah Evans
                                               Demian Clardon

  SUBJECT:     Budget Report for Valencia Project

      FOR:     [ ] action    [ ] decision    [X] information
```

Here is a summary of the attached "Valencia Project Budget Report."

Over-Budget Items:

| Labor | + $40,915 (4%) | An unbudgeted group analyst was added in January. |
| Office supplies & equipment | + $23,208 | Unbudgeted purchase of two pieces of equipment. |

Under-Budget Items:

Operating	− $32,746	Primarily because auto leasing is $19,011 under budget. Valencia was erroneously charged for one car instead of two. Several small accounts are also under budget.
Depreciation	− $18,074 (43%)	Valencia is only being charged occupancy for half of budgeted square footage. Tina Feisty in Plant Facilities is following up on this.
Metered	− $47,029 (78%)	#225—Fabrication & Services and #900—Technical Publications, budgeted at $3,502 year-to-date, have a zero balance. #445—Reproduction Costs In-house, is under budget $7,544.

Attachment: Valencia Project Budget Report

CHAPTER 12

Instructions

Writing clear instructions is one of the most difficult things to do. A noted Shakespeare scholar, G. B. Harrison, said he learned more about writing in the army than from all his schooling:

> *It is far easier to discuss Hamlet's complexes than to write orders which ensure that five working parties from five different units arrive at the right place at the right time, equipped with proper tools for the job.*
>
> *One soon learns that the most seemingly simple statement can bear two meanings, and that, when instructions are misunderstood, the fault usually lies with the wording of the original order.*

A manager sent a sample of a mailer to the printer. "Copy this exactly, and be sure to save the tear-out reply coupon," she said. She wanted to be certain that the coupons would be perforated like the sample. The large mailing went out right on schedule and the astonished manager was handed a box of blank reply coupons, carefully torn from each mailer by a staff working overtime. Moral: It is an art to give an instruction that cannot possibly be interpreted in more than one way.

Clear Thinking

No amount of skill can turn confused thinking, poor planning, or unfinished ideas into good business writing, but clumsy writing and jargon can make the simplest statement unintelligible. Look at this real example from the Office of Civil Defense during World War II:

> *Such preparations shall be made as will completely obscure all Federal buildings and non-Federal buildings occupied by the Federal Government during an air raid for any period of time from visibility by reason of internal or external illumination. Such obscuration may be obtained either by blackout construction or by termination of the illumination.*

What the writer meant was:

> *During air raids, black out all buildings used by the federal government. Either cover the windows or turn out the lights.*

President Franklin Roosevelt translated the directive like this: "Tell them that in buildings where they have to keep the work going, to put something across the windows. In buildings where they can afford to let the work stop for a while, to turn out the lights."

WHEN TO YAWN

When you are confronted with boring, confusing, or difficult communications (your own or other people's), be sure to yawn. This helps in two ways. First, it gives you valuable oxygen for the brainwork ahead. Second, it serves as a red flare, helping you notice the kind of writing you are going to avoid in the future.

TO: All Spector Employees   January 15, 1999

FROM: David Wark Griffith, Personnel

SUBJECT: Opinion Survey

The enclosed Opinion Survey is being offered to all SPECTOR employees. You
will be provided time to personally complete and return the survey the same
day you receive it. However, should personal or business reasons make this
impossible, your manager will provide time for you to complete the
questionnaire at another time. The date for final processing of survey
input is February 2, 1999.

We are introducing this internal mail approach this year in order to
evaluate a different method of survey administration. We anticipate it
will expedite the processing and feedback of survey results to all
employees and increase individual participation.

I encourage you to take advantage of the opportunity to express your
personal opinions about the many aspects of your work life. Your input
will, of course, remain totally anonymous and confidential, and your
management will receive only summarized information.

In completing the Opinion Survey, please be guided by the following.

  1. This survey is voluntary. If you do not choose to participate, simply
      return the materials in the pre-addressed, return envelope.

  2. Follow the coding instructions on the front of the coding booklet
      before beginning the survey. This coding information should be
      written in the boxes provided at the top of your answer sheet.

  3. Proceed with the survey by marking your opinions on the answer sheets
      which accompany the question booklet.

  4. If you have questions about any aspect of the survey, please call
      Personnel, Ext. 888, from 8:30 to 11:30 and 1:30 to 4:00 during the
      period of January 16 to January 30.

  5. Please RETURN THE SURVEY MATERIALS to Personnel in the pre-addressed
      envelope.

I encourage and appreciate your individual participation in the survey.
Summarized survey results will be provided by your manager as part of the
communication feedback process.

Encl.

WHAT TO DO

This writer has tried to make his memo easier to read by having a 1-2-3-4-5 sequence. This is a popular way of sorting information, but in this case it doesn't quite work.

1. The reader has *two* options. What are they?
   a.
   b.

2. Put an *a* next to any additional information about your "option a" that the reader *needs to know.* Put a *b* next to any additional information about your "option b" that the reader *needs to know.*

3. Circle any information that sounds like the writer talking to himself—things that position him but that don't affect the reader.

TO: All Spector Employees   January 15, 1999

FROM: David Wark Griffith, Personnel

SUBJECT: Opinion Survey

The enclosed Opinion Survey is being offered to all SPECTOR employees. You will be provided time to personally complete and return the survey the same day you receive it. However, should personal or business reasons make this impossible, your manager will provide time for you to complete the questionnaire at another time. The date for final processing of survey input is February 2, 1999.

We are introducing this internal mail approach this year in order to evaluate a different method of survey administration. We anticipate it will expedite the processing and feedback of survey results to all employees and increase individual participation.

I encourage you to take advantage of the opportunity to express your personal opinions about the many aspects of your work life. Your input will, of course, remain totally anonymous and confidential, and your management will receive only summarized information.

In completing the Opinion Survey, please be guided by the following.

1. This survey is voluntary. If you do not choose to participate, simply return the materials in the pre-addressed, return envelope.

2. Follow the coding instructions on the front of the coding booklet before beginning the survey. This coding information should be written in the boxes provided at the top of your answer sheet.

3. Proceed with the survey by marking your opinions on the answer sheets which accompany the question booklet.

4. If you have questions about any aspect of the survey, please call Personnel, Ext. 888, from 8:30 to 11:30 and 1:30 to 4:00 during the period of January 16 to January 30.

5. Please RETURN THE SURVEY MATERIALS to Personnel in the pre-addressed envelope.

I encourage and appreciate your individual participation in the survey. Summarized survey results will be provided by your manager as part of the communication feedback process.

Encl.

ANSWERS

1. The reader has two options:
    a. to respond to the survey
    b. not to respond to the survey

2. Supports for these two options are listed under the separate headings in our rewrite.

3. The reader really doesn't need to know that this is a new approach, or that management is evaluating a different method of survey administration, or that they anticipate it will expedite the processing and feedback of survey results of all employees and increase individual participation!

• • • •

OUR REWRITE

SUBJECT CHANGED FROM   Opinion Survey

TO   Your Response to Opinion Survey

HEADINGS: We have highlighted the most important points—either doing *this* or doing *that*.

NUMBERED SEQUENCES   can be very helpful. Unfortunately, in this memo neither item one nor item four are really part of the sequence. Reserve numbering for things that are a real series of related actions or objects: "Bring five things . . ." "Do these three things in this order . . ."

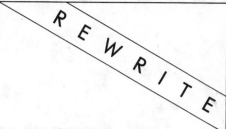

TO: All Spector Employees   DATE: January 15, 1999

FROM: David Wark Griffith, Personnel

SUBJECT: Your Response to Opinion Survey

FOR: [X] action   [ ] decision   [ ] information

The enclosed Opinion Survey is an opportunity for you to express your personal opinions about the many aspects of your work life at Spector. Your input will be totally anonymous and confidential. We will receive only a summary of your replies, which we will share with you.

This survey is voluntary.

If you choose to participate

1. Read the coding instructions before you begin and enter the correct code in the box at the top of your answer sheet.

2. Mark your opinions on the answer sheet.

3. Return the survey in the enclosed envelope by February 2.

If you do not choose to participate

Return the materials in the enclosed envelope.

Questions? Please call Personnel at Ext. 888 before January 30. Call before 11:30 or after 1:30.

Need more time? If the time you are given today to fill out the answer sheet isn't sufficient, your manager will see that you have time to do it before the February 2 deadline.

I appreciate your taking part in this survey.

Encl: Survey form

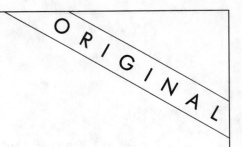

TO: MATERIALS CONTROL

FROM: THE COMMAND CENTER

RE: STAGING FREIGHT IN THE S.C.T. AREA

THE S.C.T. STAGING AREA HAS BEEN DIVIDED INTO FOUR SUB-AREAS: GROUND
FREIGHT, AIR FREIGHT, UPS, AND FEDERAL EXPRESS.

USING THE WEIGHT CHART BELOW, ALL PRODUCT IS TO BE STAGED IN ITS APPROPRIATE
AREA.

S.C.T.'s SHIPPING OUT GROUND:
1-100 LBS. GO IN THE UPS AREA
100 LBS. AND UP GO IN THE GROUND FREIGHT AREA

S.C.T.'s SHIPPING OUT AIR:
1-19 LBS. GO IN THE FEDERAL EXPRESS AREA
20 LBS. AND UP GO IN THE AIR FREIGHT AREA

ALL S.C.T.'s SHIPPING OUT "RUSH" (NEXT DAY DELIVERY) MUST BE BROUGHT UP TO
THE COMMAND CENTER FOR FURTHER EVALUATION.

THANK YOU FOR YOUR COOPERATION.

cc: S. Livingston
     L. Stanley

WHAT TO DO

This *real* memo lacks the date it was sent, the date the new procedure goes into effect, and even the writer's name if you want to ask questions. And it is in all-caps, very difficult to read.

However, it looks pretty clear—all those nice breakouts of information. How could it be clearer?

1. There are actually several ways to divide the information the writer is offering so that the reader can absorb it more easily. Choose one that would be most helpful to you if you were standing there with a package to send out:

   [ ]   by weight
   [ ]   by name of area
   [ ]   by ground or air
   [ ]   by name of freight service

2. Craft a rough chart of the information here, using the format you selected above.

TO: MATERIALS CONTROL

FROM: THE COMMAND CENTER

RE: STAGING FREIGHT IN THE S.C.T. AREA

THE S.C.T. STAGING AREA HAS BEEN DIVIDED INTO FOUR SUB-AREAS: GROUND FREIGHT, AIR FREIGHT, UPS, AND FEDERAL EXPRESS.

USING THE WEIGHT CHART BELOW, ALL PRODUCT IS TO BE STAGED IN ITS APPROPRIATE AREA.

S.C.T.'s SHIPPING OUT GROUND:
1–100 LBS. GO IN THE UPS AREA
100 LBS. AND UP GO IN THE GROUND FREIGHT AREA

S.C.T.'s SHIPPING OUT AIR:
1–19 LBS. GO IN THE FEDERAL EXPRESS AREA
20 LBS. AND UP GO IN THE AIR FREIGHT AREA

ALL S.C.T.'s SHIPPING OUT "RUSH" (NEXT DAY DELIVERY) MUST BE BROUGHT UP TO THE COMMAND CENTER FOR FURTHER EVALUATION.

THANK YOU FOR YOUR COOPERATION.

cc: S. Livingston
     L. Stanley

ANSWERS

1. We chose "by ground or air."
    [ ] by weight: You may not know the exact weight.
    [ ] by name of area: Easy to locate, but why are you there?
    [X] by ground or air: Most people have some sense of the distance and speed necessary for their package.
    [ ] by name of freight service: Useless unless you are a shipping expert.

2. Compare your chart to our rewrite. An easy-to-scan chart helps fix comparisons in people's minds.

•   •   •   •

OUR REWRITE

SUBJECT CHANGED FROM   Staging Freight in the S.C.T. Area

TO   New Staging Areas for SCT Freight

MISSING INFORMATION: We have added the date the memo was sent, the starting date, a name for the sender, and instructions to bring any questions or problems to that impressive-sounding "Command Center."

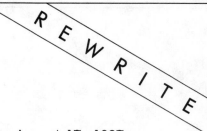

To: Materials Control   Date: August 17, 1997

From: The Command Center, J. Jones   CC: S. Livingston
                                                   L. Stanley

SUBJECT: New Staging Areas for SCT Freight

   FOR: [X] action   [ ] decision   [X] information

Starting today, use the newly marked shipping stations in the SCT
(Spector Coffee & Tea) area as follows:

Ground Shipments
1 to 100 lbs.   UPS Area
100 lbs. and up   Ground Freight Area

Air Shipments
1 to 19 lbs.   Federal Express Area
20 lbs. and up   Air Freight Area

Undecided?
Bring your package to the Command Center and we'll decide the best way for
it to go.

"RUSH" Deliveries
Bring all SCT shipping that is going out "RUSH" (next-day delivery) to the
Command Center for further evaluation.

Thanks for your cooperation.

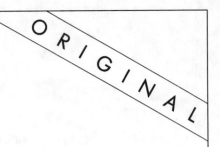

November 25, 1996

     TO: All Pension and Profit Sharing Plan Participants

   FROM: Bert Wheeler,
             Corporate Payroll & Benefits Manager

SUBJECT: Distribution of Profit Sharing Funds and Waiver of Qualified
             Joint, Survivor Annuity and Spousal Consent

Because you elected either a full cash or partial cash distribution of your profit sharing funds, you must complete the attached Waiver of Qualified Joint, Survivor Annuity and Spousal Consent form before we can release your check.

If you are not married, please complete and sign Section I and Section A.

If you are married, please complete Section II and Section A; your spouse must complete Section B. Please note that your spouse's signature is required and must be witnessed by a Notary Public or a Designated Representative of SPECTOR. As a convenience to you, Designated Representatives of the Payroll & Benefits Department will be available to witness your spouse's signature on Saturday, December 13, 1996, from 10:00 a.m. to 2:00 p.m. at Corporate headquarters, 222 Spector Avenue, Spectorville. In order for us to witness your spouse's signature, your spouse must provide a picture I.D. with signature (such as a driver's license) as proof of identity.

It is important that you complete and return this form to us as soon as possible, but no later than December 15th, in order to avoid any delay in receiving your profit sharing distribution. We are legally required to have this form completed before your funds may be released.

If you have any questions, please call the Payroll & Benefits Department at 777-7777.

Bert Wheeler

WHAT TO DO

How many letters or memos of financial instructions like this one have you received in your lifetime? It tells everything the *writer* knows about the subject, but what does the reader need to know?

1. Underline what the reader is being asked to do.

2. Put checks next to the reader's various options for doing this.

3. Write down some possible headings for these options below. (Do they suggest a way to divide the information for easier understanding?)

4. Put a star next to other informational points that the reader needs to know.

5. Put a double underscore under the deadline for responding.

WHAT WE DID

November 25, 1996

TO: All Pension and Profit Sharing Plan Participants

FROM: Bert Wheeler,
        Corporate Payroll & Benefits Manager

SUBJECT: Distribution of Profit Sharing Funds and Waiver of Qualified
         Joint, Survivor Annuity and Spousal Consent

Because you elected either a full cash or partial cash distribution of your
profit sharing funds, you must complete the attached Waiver of Qualified
Joint, Survivor Annuity and Spousal Consent form before we can release your
check.

If you are not married, please complete and sign Section I and Section A.

If you are married, please complete Section II and Section A; your spouse
must complete Section B. Please note that your spouse's signature is
required and must be witnessed by a Notary Public or a Designated
Representative of SPECTOR. As a convenience to you, Designated
Representatives of the Payroll & Benefits Department will be available to
witness your spouse's signature on Saturday, December 13, 1996, from 10:00
a.m. to 2:00 p.m. at Corporate headquarters, 222 Spector Avenue,
Spectorville. In order for us to witness your spouse's signature, your
spouse must provide a picture I.D. with signature (such as a driver's
license) as proof of identity.

It is important that you complete and return this form to us as soon as
possible, but no later than December 15th, in order to avoid any delay in
receiving your profit sharing distribution. We are legally required to
have this form completed before your funds may be released.

If you have any questions, please call the Payroll & Benefits Department at
777-7777.

Bert Wheeler

ANSWERS

1. The reader is being asked to "complete the attached Waiver" (first sentence).

2. Options: married/unmarried. Also use of outside or company notary.

3. Headings should suggest ways to chart the information for easier reading. Our choice for headings is in the rewrite.

4. The reader needs to know:
   Paragraph three: Spouse's signature must be notarized.
   A representative will be available to witness spouses' signatures.
   Spouses must sign the form in the representative's presence and provide a picture ID with signature.
   Paragraph four: The form must be completed no later than December 15.

5. Deadline is mentioned in paragraph four!

•   •   •   •

OUR REWRITE

SUBJECT
CHANGED FROM   Distribution of Profit Sharing
                Funds and Waiver of Qualified
                Joint, Survivor Annuity and
                Spousal Consent

        TO   How to Get Your Profit Sharing
              Funds

ATTACHMENT   listed at bottom of page.

```
    TO:     All Pension and Profit       DATE:    November 25, 1996
            Sharing Plan Participants

    FROM:   Bert Wheeler, Corporate Payroll & Benefits Manager

 SUBJECT:   How to Get Your Profit Sharing Funds

    FOR:    [X] action    [ ] decision    [ ] information
```

Before we can release your check, you must complete the attached "Waiver of Qualified Joint, Survivor Annuity, and Spousal Consent" form. Please return it to us as soon as possible, but no later than <u>December 15</u>.

This is necessary because you elected either a full or partial cash payment from your profit sharing funds. We are legally required to have this form completed before giving you your check.

<u>If you are not married</u>, please complete and sign:
    Section I
    Section A

<u>If you are married</u>, you and your spouse should complete and sign:
    Section II
    Section A
    Section B

 Your spouse's signature must be witnessed by a Notary Public or a
 Designated Representative of Spector's Payroll & Benefits Department.

<u>Free Notary Services</u>: As a convenience to you, Spector is offering free notary services on Saturday, December 13, from 10 A.M. to 2 P.M. at the corporate headquarters, 222 Spector Avenue, Spectorville. Your spouse must bring a picture ID with signature (such as a driver's license) as proof of identity.

If you have any questions, please call 777-7777.

ATTACHMENT: Form—"Waiver of Qualified Joint, Survivor Annuity, and
            Spousal Consent"

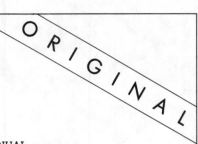

CORPORATE CONTROLLER'S POLICY MANUAL

1. <u>PURPOSE</u>
To provide guidelines to management for their response to
recommendations on accounting and operational systems and controls
prepared by the Internal Audit Department or Independent Public
Accounts.

2. <u>SCOPE</u>
This policy is applicable to all organizational units of Spector.

3. <u>Definitions</u>
   A. Responsible Party—The term Responsible Party includes the
      Controller—Corporate Reporting and Policy, the Controller—
      Operations, the Controllers of the Operating Groups and Regional
      Divisions and the Directors of the U.S. and International Groups.
   B. Local Management—The term Local Management refers to all
      affiliate, division, area, group, and corporate department
      personnel <u>except</u> Group Executive Vice Presidents, any Responsible
      Party, the Corporate Chief Accounting Officer, the Corporate Chief
      Financial Officer, and the Corporate President.
   C. Red Letter Report—The term Red Letter Report refers to the
      Management Letter issued by G.T. Fitzherbert & Co. upon completion
      of an audit. A Red Letter issued to a subsidiary is referred to as an
      Affiliate Red Letter.
   D. Controller's Letter—The term Controller's Letter refers to the
      G.T. Fitzherbert & Co. reports issued to the Controller—Corporate
      Reporting & Policy, the Controller—Operations and the Controller—
      International Group including recommendations not considered
      significant enough to be included in the Red Letter issued to the
      Audit Committee.

4. <u>POLICY</u>
   A. <u>Internal Audit Reports—Findings of Special Interest</u>
      The Internal Audit Department routinely performs financial and
      operational audits during the course of the year. The resulting
      reports discuss their findings with recommendations for corrective
      action and/or improvement. The Internal Audit Reports are submitted
      to the Local Management with whom the audit finding is being raised
      as well as to the appropriate Responsible Party. Local Management

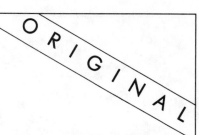

must generally respond to the appropriate Responsible Party and the Internal Audit within 60 days of the date of the report.

1) When Local Management agrees to implement a recommendation in an Internal Audit Report
    Local Management has a period not to exceed 60 days from the date of the report to implement their recommendation and notify the appropriate Responsible Party and the Internal Audit Department that action has been taken. The Responsible Party must follow up, if corrective action is not taken in this time period.

    NOTE: In case of a significant implementation project, the 60 day period may be extended with the approval of the Responsible Party.

2) When Local Management rejects a recommendation in an Internal Audit Report
    The Responsible Party must be advised of the rejection
    a) If the Responsible Party overrules the rejection, Local Management has a maximum of 60 days from the date the rejection is overruled to implement the recommendation and notify the appropriate Responsible Party. The Internal Audit Department should be notified by Local Management at the beginning of the implementation and also upon completion. The Responsible Party must follow up, if corrective action is not taken in this time period.

        NOTE: In the case of a significant implementation project, the 60 day period may be extended with the approval of the Responsible Party.

    b) If the Responsible Party agrees with Local Management's rejection of the recommendation, he must notify the Internal Audit Department of his position.

        (1) If the Internal Audit Department agrees that implementation of a recommendation is not necessary, the Internal Audit Department must write a memo to the Responsible Party documenting the change in position.
        (2) If the Internal Audit Department insists that corrective action be taken, the Responsible Party must obtain the following approvals for his rejection.

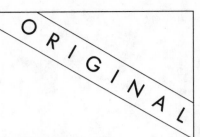

(i) the Group Executive Vice President (except Controller—
Corporate Reporting and Policy) and

(ii) the Corporate Chief Accounting Officer

c) If the Group Executive Vice President or the Corporate Chief
Accounting Officer feels that implementation of the
recommendation is necessary, the Responsible Party is notified.
The Responsible Party then allows Local Management a maximum of
60 days from the date the rejection is overruled to implement the
recommendation and notify the Responsible Party. The Internal
Audit Department should be notified by Local Management at the
beginning of the implementation and also upon completion. The
Responsible Party must follow up, if corrective action is not
taken in this time period.

NOTE: In the case of a significant implementation project, the
60 day period may be extended with the approval of the
Responsible Party.

d) If the Corporate Chief Accounting Officer feels that
implementation of the recommendation is necessary, but the
Group Executive Vice President does not, the Group Executive
Vice President can appeal to the Corporate Chief Operating
Officer (and should notify the Corporate Chief Accounting
Officer of such action). If there is no resolution at this point,
the Corporate Chief Financial Officer, and, if necessary, both
the Corporate Chief Financial Officer and Corporate Chief
Operating Officer can appeal to the Corporate President and
finally to the Audit Committee.

The Corporate Chief Accounting Officer should notify the
Internal Audit Department at the beginning of this appeal
process.

e) If the Group Executive Vice President and the Corporate Chief
Accounting Officer agree with the rejection of the
recommendation, the Internal Audit Department must be notified
of all such rejections by the Responsible Party.

WHAT TO DO

Here is a real section of a Manual of Procedures. Does it look familiar? Do you instantly know what you are supposed to do?

The writer realized that the procedures being described were frequently of the either/or variety and tried to show this by putting the information in a classical outline format. This resulted in the sub-sub-subcategories becoming skinny ribbons of text on the final page.

1. Suggest a topic heading for this material.

2. Put a check wherever the writer starts to discuss a new option. Jot down possible headings for each block of information.

3. Do readers need to know the purpose of this procedure?

4. Do readers need to know the scope of this policy?

CORPORATE CONTROLLER'S POLICY MANUAL

1. **PURPOSE**
   To provide guidelines to management for their response to recommendations on accounting and operational systems and controls prepared by the Internal Audit Department or Independent Public Accounts.

2. **SCOPE**
   This policy is applicable to all organizational units of Spector.

3. **Definitions**
   A. Responsible Party—The term Responsible Party includes the Controller—Corporate Reporting and Policy, the Controller—Operations, the Controllers of the Operating Groups and Regional Divisions and the Directors of the U.S. and International Groups.
   B. Local Management—The term Local Management refers to all affiliate, division, area, group, and corporate department personnel *except* Group Executive Vice Presidents, any Responsible Party, the Corporate Chief Accounting Officer, the Corporate Chief Financial Officer, and the Corporate President.
   C. Red Letter Report—The term Red Letter Report refers to the Management Letter issued by G.T. Fitzherbert & Co. upon completion of an audit. A Red Letter issued to a subsidiary is referred to as an Affiliate Red Letter.
   D. Controller's Letter—The term Controller's Letter refers to the G.T. Fitzherbert & Co. reports issued to the Controller—Corporate Reporting and Policy, the Controller—Operations and the Controller—International Group including recommendations not considered significant enough to be included in the Red Letter issued to the Audit Committee.

4. **POLICY**
   A. Internal Audit Reports—Findings of Special Interest
   The Internal Audit Department routinely performs financial and operational audits during the course of the year. The resulting reports discuss their findings with recommendations for corrective action and/or improvement. The Internal Audit Reports are submitted to the Local Management with whom the audit finding is being raised as well as to the appropriate Responsible Party. Local Management

must generally respond to the appropriate Responsible Party and the Internal Audit within 60 days of the date of the report.

1) When Local Management agrees to implement a recommendation in an Internal Audit Report
   Local Management has a period not to exceed 60 days from the date of the report to implement their recommendation and notify the appropriate Responsible Party and the Internal Audit Department that action has been taken. The Responsible Party must follow up, if corrective action is not taken in this time period.

   NOTE: In case of a significant implementation project, the 60 day period may be extended with the approval of the Responsible Party.

2) When Local Management rejects a recommendation in an Internal Audit Report
   The Responsible Party must be advised of the rejection
   a) If the Responsible Party overrules the rejection, Local Management has a maximum of 60 days from the date the rejection is overruled to implement the recommendation and notify the appropriate Responsible Party. The Internal Audit Department should be notified by Local Management at the beginning of the implementation and also upon completion. The Responsible Party must follow up, if corrective action is not taken in this time period.

      NOTE: In the case of a significant implementation project, the 60 day period may be extended with the approval of the Responsible Party.

   b) If the Responsible Party agrees with Local Management's rejection of the recommendation, he must notify the Internal Audit Department of his position.

      (1) If the Internal Audit Department agrees that implementation of a recommendation is not necessary, the Internal Audit Department must write a memo to the Responsible Party documenting the change in position.
      (2) If the Internal Audit Department insists that corrective action be taken, the Responsible Party must obtain the following approvals for his rejection.

         (i) the Group Executive Vice President (except Controller—Corporate Reporting and Policy) and
         (ii) the Corporate Chief Accounting Officer

   c) If the Group Executive Vice President or the Corporate Chief Accounting Officer feels that implementation of the recommendation is necessary, the Responsible Party is notified. The Responsible Party then allows Local Management a maximum of 60 days from the date the rejection is overruled to implement the recommendation and notify the Responsible Party. The Internal Audit Department should be notified by Local Management at the beginning of the implementation and also upon completion. The Responsible Party must follow up, if corrective action is not taken in this time period.

      NOTE: In the case of a significant implementation project, the 60 day period may be extended with the approval of the Responsible Party.

   d) If the Corporate Chief Accounting Officer feels that implementation of the recommendation is necessary, but the Group Executive Vice President does not, the Group Executive Vice President can appeal to the Corporate Chief Operating Officer (and should notify the Corporate Chief Accounting Officer of such action). If there is no resolution at this point, the Corporate Chief Financial Officer, and, if necessary, both the Corporate Chief Financial Officer and Corporate Chief Operating Officer can appeal to the Corporate President and finally to the Audit Committee.

      The Corporate Chief Accounting Officer should notify the Internal Audit Department at the beginning of this appeal process.

   e) If the Group Executive Vice President and the Corporate Chief Accounting Officer agree with the rejection of the recommendation, the Internal Audit Department must be notified of all such rejections by the Responsible Party.

ANSWERS

1. Section heading is: Responding to Audit Recommendations

2. See headings in rewrite on opposite page.

3. Readers probably don't need to know the purpose of this procedure. This statement, intended as a guideline for the writer, can be summarized in the heading.

4. Readers probably don't need to know the scope of this policy. Any exceptions can be covered in an opening statement or within the text of the directives.

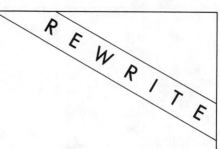

CORPORATE POLICY MANUAL

CORPORATE CONTROLLER'S POLICY MANUAL
RESPONDING TO AUDIT RECOMMENDATIONS

<u>Response by Local Management</u>

When Local Management receives audit recommendations, either from the Internal Audit Department or from independent public accounts, it has 15 days to advise its Responsible Party (see definitions on page ____) whether it accepts or rejects them.

> <u>If it accepts</u> the recommendation, Local Management has 60 days from the date of receiving the report to implement the recommendation and to report that it has done so to the appropriate Responsible Party and to the Internal Audit Department. (The Responsible Party may grant an extension for major implementations.)

> <u>If it rejects</u> the recommendation, Local Management should report this to the Responsible Party within ____ days. The Responsible Party then has 15 days to agree with the rejection or to overrule it.

<u>Response by Responsible Party to Rejection</u>

If the Responsible Party <u>overrules the rejection</u> by Local Management, there is no further appeal and Local Management has 60 days from that date to implement the audit recommendation.

If the Responsible Party <u>agrees with the rejection</u> by Local Management, the Responsible Party must notify the Internal Audit Department of his/her position within ____ days.

<u>Response by the Internal Audit Department</u>

If the Internal Audit Department <u>agrees with the rejection</u> and feels the requested change is not necessary, it must write a memo to the Responsible Party confirming their position.

If the Internal Audit Department <u>overrules the rejection</u> by Local Management that has been seconded by the Responsible Party, the Responsible Party can appeal to both the Group Executive Vice President and the Corporate Chief Accounting Officer. Both of them must agree with the rejection in order to overrule the Internal Audit Department.

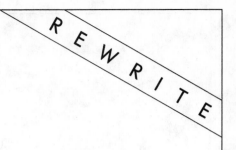

<u>Further Appeals</u>

If the Group Executive Vice President <u>supports the recommendation</u> of the Internal Audit Department, the recommendation will be implemented without further appeal within 60 days of the rejection. Local Management notifies Internal Auditing and the Responsible Party and proceeds as above.

If the Group Executive Vice President <u>disagrees with the recommendation</u> of the Internal Audit Department, but the Corporate Chief Accounting Officer supports it, then each can appeal to higher authority: the Group Executive Vice President appeals to the Corporate Chief Operating Officer; the Corporate Chief Accounting Officer appeals to the Corporate Chief Financial Officer.

If the Corporate Chief Operating Officer and the Corporate Chief Financial Officer cannot agree, they can in turn appeal to the Corporate President, and finally to the Audit Committee.

*   *   *   *   *

[Put all definitions alphabetically at the end of the manual.]

<u>Controller's Letter</u>   A separate report prepared by G. T. Fitzherbert & Co. that is issued to:
    Controller—Corporate Reporting & Policy
    Controller—Operations
    Controller—International Group
It includes recommendations not considered significant enough to be included in the Red Letter issued to the Audit Committee.

<u>Local Management</u>   The term refers to:
  All affiliate, division, area, group, and corporate department
  personnel
  <u>except</u>
    any Responsible Party
    Group Executive Vice Presidents
    Corporate Chief Accounting Officer
    Corporate Chief Financial Officer
    Corporate President

<u>Red Letter Report</u>   The Management Letter issued by G. T. Fitzherbert & Co. when it has completed the audit. (A Red Letter issued to a subsidiary is referred to as an Affiliate Red Letter.)

<u>Responsible Party</u>   The term includes:
    Controller—Corporate Reporting and Policy
    Controller—Operations
    Controllers of the Operating Groups and Regional Divisions
    Directors of the U.S. and International Groups

CHAPTER 13

Zingers

Finally we come to the innocent-looking memo called the *zinger*. When you sit down to write, do you ever imagine that each word might be worth $1 million? Probably not, but that's what is happening more and more frequently in the courtrooms of America.

Some corporate memos have brought legal settlements that cost the defendants as much as $1 million a word or more. Other memos have produced embarrassment, loss of credibility, and jail sentences.

- The Ford Motor Company, in the now-classic Pinto case, was ordered to pay a California teenager $128 million in damages after his attorney presented internal Ford memos that showed Ford's own testing had turned up the Pinto design defect that injured the boy, but the company had decided not to modify the Pinto gas tanks because it would cost ten dollars per car.

- Pacific Gas & Electric was ordered to pay $7.5 million to an independent filmmaker who had made an unfavorable documentary about the big utility. A judge ruled that a memo in which a PG&E executive ordered subordinates to see that the filmmaker never worked again showed "malice."

- A regional inspector general for the Environmental Protection Agency sent a memo advising his subordinates to destroy and conceal information "which could prove embarrassing." He wrote: "We have to start thinking about what to get rid of before the FOIA [Freedom of Information Act] request catches us with our pants down."

- American Airlines was ordered to pay more than $2 million in penalties for concealing the whereabouts of a maintenance report prepared after the crash of a DC-10 that killed 273 persons.

- In antitrust litigation between Berkey Photo and Eastman Kodak, one of Kodak's lawyers was disbarred and sent to jail for concealing documents.

- A confidential memo containing the frank personal opinions of TV newsman Bryant Gumble about a popular coworker was leaked to the press, making front-page headlines.

No Secrets

This is the age of the tape recorder and the copy machine. There is no longer any such thing as confidentiality. Corporate writing today must anticipate both the intended and the unintended audience. Zingers can lurk in filing cabinets like UXBs—unexploded bombs—awaiting their day in the spotlight.

Internal security classifications such as "confidential" can't keep sensitive documents out of the hands of people intent on litigation, regulation, or retaliation. Ask yourself, "How would these words taste if I had to eat them in front of a jury or the president of my company's largest customer or competitor?"

This doesn't mean you stop writing or you stop telling the truth—to be effective, you have to respond to sensitive issues—but you can learn to do it without creating a zinger.

Whenever you write something critical, a red light should go on in your head. Let's say that you notice a real problem that should be dealt with at once. You immediately send a memo.

NOT: Someone is going to get killed.
BUT: The loading door must be fixed immediately.

NOT: Those thieves are robbing us blind.
BUT: We have severe shortages.

Don't try to conceal unpleasant facts or fail to report dangerous situations. The courts take a dim view of that too. Just use your common sense and get legal advice if you're unsure.

NOT:	An unaccountable mixture of gases caused the building to become loose on its foundation.
BUT:	There was an explosion.
NOT:	There is an increase in reportage due to altered criteria in meeting the standards of the XYZ Board.
BUT:	Quality Control reports more errors.

These are obfuscations. They may conceal your real meaning, but not for long.

CYA Memos

A variation on the zinger is the CYA memo. This is a valiant and self-righteous attempt to point the finger elsewhere so that history will later show that *it's not my fault!* Writing a CYA memo is a very human act and can spring even from the noblest motives. What the writers forget is that while they are busy trying to cover their own backsides, they are baring someone else's. CYA memos can also backfire because some readers may see the writer as incompetent, disloyal, and/or engaged in a cover-up. Remember that any documented infighting lays the whole organization open to attack from the outside and can come back to haunt you in years to come.

Writing in Anger

We never write more brilliantly than when we are angry. Anger is natural, even laudable, in many situations. But if you must write when you are mad, do it by hand. Don't dictate it and don't make a copy. Take the angry words home and put them under your pillow overnight. In the morning, tear them up, burn the pieces, and flush the ashes down the toilet.

Then sit down and write *what the reader needs to know*—the words that will go to work to resolve the problem. You will feel immensely better for having said all those wickedly clever things and your career prospects will be substantially enhanced because you had the wisdom not to send them.

WHAT TO DO

Following are three disguised examples of real zingers. Each may get a response that the writer didn't bargain for.

Don't rewrite these memos. Just go through them and underline anything that has the potential to cause future trouble. Then compare what you underlined with what we did.

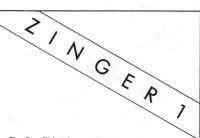
ZINGER 1

ATLANTA PROJECTS DIVISION
Spector Corporation of America

August 24, 1998

cc: S.J. Winters
     T.C. Hamilton
     J.M. Munson
     E.R. Dugan
     J.M. Wit
     P.P. Summerfield
     J. Yamamoto
     E.R. Rabb
     S.T. Johaneson
     P.T. Strasburg
     F. Friederich
     O.G. Gundersen

G.H. Hanson, Manager
Quality Assurance

SUBJECT: PEACHTREE PROJECT QUALITY ASSURANCE

The Peachtree project has a continuing Quality Assurance problem with the
products manufactured and shipped by your Department. Stated very briefly,
there continues to be a substantial quantity of errors across several vital
quality–related documents. These errors are occurring primarily in
documents which supply ship–short items for Peachtree in the field. The key
documents are: RRT, SSIS, and TAG (all for ship–short material). The
problem caused by errors, omissions, or inconsistencies in these documents
comes to a head at the job site. Upon receipt of the hardware at the site,
the owner inventories the shipment and makes a cross check against the
appropriate RRT, SSIS, and TAG. If disconnects appear, he places the
hardware in quarantine and advises our site forces to straighten out our
paperwork. This takes valuable time. Almost without exception, ship–short
hardware is overdue when it arrives at the site and to have it placed in
quarantine upon arrival is disastrous. Further, valuable SPECTOR resources
are expended just to unscramble the paperwork.

I have met with Messrs. Winters, Hamilton, Munson, and Dugan. To my
knowledge no one seems responsible or responsive to accept the above
problem and its total context from start to finish. To assist you in further
understanding this problem, attached are two detailed memos listing recent
Peachtree software problems.

Peachtree has substantial amounts of equipment yet to be shipped, so
attention to and resolution of the above problem is requested. My staff and
the Peachtree site staff are available to work with you. I would be pleased
to hear from you on your plans to address this request.

G.G. Fenster, Project Manager
Peachtree Project

ZINGER 1

Zinger words and phrases are underlined in the version on the opposite page.

This writer wants to make an impression and he probably will. Even if this memo never ends up in court, its implication that he works with nincompoops may make him lots of enemies.

Of course the Quality Assurance manager needs to know about the chaos at the job site, but a well-documented request for assistance without all the red-flag words would be just as effective. Better yet, if anyone ever sues because of delays in the project, a thoughtful memo would show how hard Spector worked to overcome the problems.

ATLANTA PROJECTS DIVISION
Spector Corporation of America   cc: S.J. Winters
                                                         T.C. Hamilton
August 24, 1998   J.M. Munson
                                                         E.R. Dugan
                                                         J.M. Wit
                                                         P.P. Summerfield
                                                         J. Yamamoto
                                                         E.R. Rabb
                                                         S.T. Johaneson
                                                         P.T. Strasburg
                                                         F. Friederich
                                                         O.G. Gundersen

G.H. Hanson, Manager
Quality Assurance

SUBJECT: PEACHTREE PROJECT QUALITY ASSURANCE

The Peachtree project has a continuing Quality Assurance problem with the
products manufactured and shipped by your Department. Stated very briefly,
there continues to be a substantial quantity of errors across several vital
quality-related documents. These errors are occurring primarily in
documents which supply ship-short items for Peachtree in the field. The key
documents are: RRT, SSIS, and TAG (all for ship-short material). The
problem caused by errors, omissions, or inconsistencies in these documents
comes to a head at the job site. Upon receipt of the hardware at the site,
the owner inventories the shipment and makes a cross check against the
appropriate RRT, SSIS, and TAG. If disconnects appear, he places the
hardware in quarantine and advises our site forces to straighten out our
paperwork. This takes valuable time. Almost without exception, ship-short
hardware is overdue when it arrives at the site and to have it placed in
quarantine upon arrival is disastrous. Further, valuable SPECTOR resources
are expended just to unscramble the paperwork.

I have met with Messrs. Winters, Hamilton, Munson, and Dugan. To my
knowledge, no one seems responsible or responsive to accept the above
problem and its total context from start to finish. To assist you in further
understanding this problem, attached are two detailed memos listing recent
Peachtree software problems.

Peachtree has substantial amounts of equipment yet to be shipped, so
attention to and resolution of the above problem is requested. My staff and
the Peachtree site staff are available to work with you. I would be pleased
to hear from you on your plans to address this request.

G.G. Fenster, Project Manager
Peachtree Project

Everything you write has two audiences: the intended and the unintended. Remember that angry words are like pizza. They taste awful the next day.

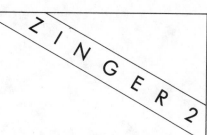

```
        TO:    Constance Talmadge        DATE:    September 21, 1998

      FROM:    Richard Barthelmess

   SUBJECT:    BIRMINGHAM'S SILVER-SLEEP PERMITS
```

In a previous progress meeting last May with Birmingham Builders, we have
told our customer that SPECTOR's negotiations with the Chinese government
to obtain land and building permits for the 73 Silver-Sleep Motel sites is
going well. They were also told that they would be billed for the whole
effort at the end of phase 1—establishing the details of the arrangements
with the various government agencies—before the end of 1998.

Yesterday Robert Harron informed me that Silver-Sleep is not even on
SPECTOR's work list in 1998 and that SPECTOR has no resources for this
project for the next couple of years.

Our credibility on this subject has already been very poor. I cannot
imagine how they are going to take this. Permits' job is to help our
customers minimize the time needed to acquire the permits and to keep them
reasonably happy. If the situation is really as Harron says, we have just
taken a giant step BACKWARDS.

Can you advise me what I can do to protect my SPECTOR emblem in front of
Birmingham and still get the job done?

CC: S. Owen/A. Paget
     L. Gish
     M. Cooper
     E. Pallette
     M. Marsh

```
```

ZINGER 2

Zinger words and phrases are underlined in the version on the opposite page.

This memo describes a crisis. Spector has a lot of trouble and the writer has yelled "Fire!"

Now imagine this memo in the hands of Birmingham Builders when they sue. How would you rewrite it to solve the problem without creating a new one?

Maybe something like this:

> Please budget $ _____ immediately for the Silver-Sleep Permit Acquisition Program.

Or:

> Licensing needs two additional personnel immediately to handle the Silver-Sleep Permit Acquisition Program.

Point out the problem by offering a solution if you can. This shows that both you and your company are on the ball.

TO: Constance Talmadge   DATE: September 21, 1998

FROM: Richard Barthelmess

SUBJECT: BIRMINGHAM'S SILVER—SLEEP PERMITS

In a previous progress meeting last May with Birmingham Builders, we have told our customer that SPECTOR's negotiations with the Chinese government to obtain land and building permits for the 73 Silver—Sleep Motel sites is going well. They were also told that they would be billed for the whole effort at the end of phase 1—establishing the details of the arrangements with the various government agencies—before the end of 1998.

Yesterday Robert Harron informed me that Silver—Sleep is not even on SPECTOR's work list in 1998 and that SPECTOR has no resources for this project for the next couple of years.

Our credibility on this subject has already been very poor. I cannot imagine how they are going to take this. Permits' job is to help our customers minimize the time needed to acquire the permits and to keep them reasonably happy. If the situation is really as Harron says, we have just taken a giant step BACKWARDS.

Can you advise me what I can do to protect my SPECTOR emblem in front of Birmingham and still get the job done?

CC: S. Owen/A. Paget
     L. Gish
     M. Cooper
     E. Pallette
     M. Marsh

Z I N G E R 3

TO: Distribution   DATE: January 12, 1998

FROM: Ernst Lubitsch

SUBJECT: Labor Relations Workshop   DEPT: Industrial
                                           Relations

CONFIDENTIAL

Some of us have discussed, in the past, the advisability of our conducting Labor Relations training. With the recent personnel reorganization, it seems that now would be a good time for the workshop.

You are invited to attend a workshop that we have developed for field management personnel on "How to Deal with the Union." Subjects addressed include:

- Labor—Management Relations Principles
- Collective Bargaining Process
- Management Rights
- Grievance Procedure Administration
- Resolving Legitimate Grievances
- Corrective Discipline—just cause

The approach of the workshop is practical and "hands on," utilizing case studies of actual incidents to encourage discussion and participation of the group. Most case studies have no "correct" solution. Much of the material covered is also applicable to non—union environments.

We have scheduled the workshop for Tuesday, January 27, from 10:00 a.m. until 3:30 p.m. (with a one and a half hour lunch break) in Room T—654. I have enclosed a copy of our Schenectady union contract which you should read and study in detail prior to the meeting, since it will serve as the basis for case study discussion. Please protect its confidentiality and bring it to the workshop with you.

Unless we hear from you otherwise, we look forward to seeing you January 27.

DISTRIBUTION:
Maurice Chevalier	Charles Ruggles	Charles Judels
Jeanette MacDonald	Virginia Bruce	Barbara Leonard
Miriam Hopkins	Claudette Colbert	Florine McKinney
Herbert Marshall	Betty Grable	Donald Novis
Jennifer Jones	Margaret O'Brien	George Davis
Peter Lawford	Robert Young	Bess Flowers
E.E. Horton	Jack Buchanan	Lili Damita
George Barbier	ZaSu Pitts	Pierre Etchpare
Una Merkel	Tyler Brook	Andre Cheron
Reginald Owen	Josephine Dunn	Richard Carle

ZINGER 3

Zinger words and phrases are underlined in the version on the opposite page.

The problem here is confidentiality. How can a memo sent to thirty people hope to remain out of the hands of the "enemy"? Creating this adversary position on paper, whether or not it exists in real life, gives your opponent a strong handle on your actions.

If the contract is really confidential, it shouldn't be duplicated and sent to thirty people! Hand out numbered copies at the meeting and take each copy back before everyone leaves.

Even better, *write for all readers*—the union as well as management. The title of this workshop could even be changed to "Working with the Union" instead of "How to Deal with the Union." The latter may reflect how everyone feels, but the former says the same thing and can't offend anyone, even the union president.

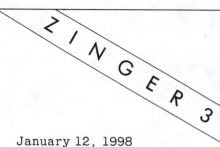
ZINGER 3

TO: Distribution   DATE: January 12, 1998

FROM: Ernst Lubitsch

SUBJECT: Labor Relations Workshop   DEPT: Industrial
                                             Relations

CONFIDENTIAL

Some of us have discussed, in the past, the advisability of our conducting Labor Relations training. With the recent personnel reorganization, it seems that now would be a good time for the workshop.

You are invited to attend a workshop that we have developed for field management personnel on "How to Deal with the Union." Subjects addressed include:

- Labor—Management Relations Principles
- Collective Bargaining Process
- Management Rights
- Grievance Procedure Administration
- Resolving Legitimate Grievances
- Corrective Discipline—just cause

The approach of the workshop is practical and "hands on," utilizing case studies of actual incidents to encourage discussion and participation of the group. Most case studies have no "correct" solution. Much of the material covered is also applicable to non—union environments.

We have scheduled the workshop for Tuesday, January 27, from 10:00 a.m. until 3:30 p.m. (with a one and a half hour lunch break) in Room T—654. I have enclosed a copy of our Schenectady union contract which you should read and study in detail prior to the meeting, since it will serve as the basis for case study discussion. Please protect its confidentiality and bring it to the workshop with you.

Unless we hear from you otherwise, we look foward to seeing you January 27.

DISTRIBUTION:
Maurice Chevalier	Charles Ruggles	Barbara Leonard	E.E. Horton
Jeanette MacDonald	Virginia Bruce	Florine McKinney	Una Merkel
Miriam Hopkins	Claudette Colbert	Donald Novis	Betty Grable
Herbert Marshall	Margaret O'Brien	George Davis	ZaSu Pitts
Jennifer Jones	Robert Young	Bess Flowers	Tyler Brook
Peter Lawford	Jack Buchanan	Pierre Etchpare	Lili Damita
George Barbier	Josephine Dunn	Andre Cheron	
Reginald Owen	Charles Judels	Richard Carle	